"Information through Innovation"

Contributors

The Publisher would like to express great appreciation to those individuals that contributed to the overall development of the STAR Series.

Joseph Dennin
Fairfield University

Edward Harms
Interactive Business Systems, Inc.

Philip J. Judd
Napier & Judd, Inc.

H. Albert Napier
Rice University

Kathleen Stewart
Moraine Valley Community College

Patrice Gapen
Laramie County Community College

Mary Last
Grand Valley State University

Patricia McMahon
Moraine Valley Community College

Philip J. Pratt
Grand Valley State University

Lotus 1-2-3 Release 2.3

A volume in the Boyd & Fraser STAR Series

H. Albert Napier
Rice University

Philip J. Judd
Napier & Judd, Inc.

boyd & fraser publishing company

Credits:

Acquisitions Editor: James H. Edwards
Production Coordinator: Pat Stephan
Marketing Manager: Christopher Will
Manufacturing Coordinator: Dean Sherman
Composition: Gex, Inc.
Cover Design: Hannus Design, Inc.

A Division of South-Western Publishing Company
Danvers, MA 01923

Manufactured in the United States of America.

The Star Series is printed on recycled, acid-free paper that meets Environmental Protection Agency standards.

ISBN: 0-87835-836-6

1 2 3 4 5 6 7 8 9 10 DH 5 4 3 2

Brief Table of Contents

Contents

Editor's Foreword

This book is one of many in the Boyd & Fraser *Software Training and Reference (STAR) Series*. The manuals in this Series are intended to provide an exceptionally innovative approach to learning popular application software programs, while at the same time providing a source for future reference—so that skills learned can be applied to constantly changing activities.

The overall development of the STAR Series is based upon the following principles:

- In order for any application software manual to be effective, it must be organized with the outlook or orientation of a novice user in mind. A novice intuitively approaches a program from the perspective of what he or she would like "to do" or accomplish, rather than from the command perspective of experienced users. *Thus the STAR Series utilizes a selection of topics oriented toward the novice user.*

- The various application software programs within the same general category (i. e., word processing, spreadsheet, database) have some underlying concepts in common. If users understand these common concepts, they will more likely take greater advantage of the associated program features. In addition, they will have less difficulty implementing the concepts within some different future program environment. Although the "how to" of a particular program feature may change or evolve, the "why" and "when" are less likely to do so. That is, while particular application software skills are often not transferrable between programs, the underlying concepts are. *Thus each topic within the STAR Series begins with a conceptual discussion.*

- There is no substitute for "learning by doing." Complete understanding of the concepts-skill linkage can only really be achieved through hands-on activity. *Thus each STAR Series topic centers around a hands-on tutorial application, highlighting the skill(s) necessary to implement the program feature.*

- Completion of a particular example alone, however, is insufficient for understanding the various nuances of a skill. *Thus relatively extensive exercises and problems, as well as reference material applicable to generalized situations, are provided within each STAR Series manual.*

- In most other tutorial-based software training manuals, the actual keystroke activities required to accomplish a tutorial are all too often lost in the surrounding explanatory material. Many users of these manuals become confused and frustrated. *Thus the STAR Series provides clear, easily distinguishable tutorial steps and directions.*

Each manual within the STAR Series is organized in the same consistent format. The selection of end-user-oriented topics focuses on those most fundamental to the effective use of the program. In addition, each manual within the same general application software category is organized as similarly as possible, while still allowing for individual program variations.

Each topic begins with a conceptual discussion of the selected program features. This **concepts section** defines the feature and presents its usefulness and applicability. The conceptual discussion is followed by a complete keystroke-by-keystroke **tutorial section**. Each action step is easily identified, and numerous screen images provide both useful "status checks" and reassuring positive reinforcement.

Following the tutorial section of the topic presentation is the **procedure summary section**. Procedure summaries not only provide useful review of the required implementation procedures or skills, but also serve as a general keystroke reference for applying those skills to future activities.

Throughout the topic presentation are numerous **tips** that include short items of interest, alternative methods for feature implementation, reference to associated topics, and advice on how to avoid common mistakes or overcome common difficulties. Concluding each topic is an **exercise section** for further hands-on skill development.

Each STAR Series manual is divided into three or more parts, each of which concludes with a **checkpoint**. The checkpoints contain numerous "What You Should Know" items designed to emphasize what can be accomplished within the particular program environment. The checkpoints also contain review questions and problems of intermediate difficulty, focusing on material covered up to that checkpoint. Each manual concludes with a **comprehensive problem** that integrates many of the program features within a single application.

DOS Coverage

To keep the overall length (and price) of each STAR Series manual down to a reasonable level, and to avoid the possibly unnecessary repetition of fundamental DOS concepts and skills, DOSscoverage for the Series is provided separately in a single stand-alone text. An inexpensive sixty-four page booklet also published by Boyd & Fraser, *DOS Essentials*, by Rod B. Southworth, provides this coverage.

Instructor's Materials

A comprehensive *Instructor's Manual* is available for use in conjunction with each STAR Series offering. These contain topic overviews, key terms, lecture notes, software suggestions, solutions to all exercises and problems, answers to checkpoint review questions, additional comprehensive exercises and solutions, and over 250 test questions. Also available is an *Instructor's Resource Disk* that contains tutorial, exercise, and problem files in various stages of completion.

Series Philosophy — Diversity and Currency

Boyd & Fraser intends to extend the STAR Series to include coverage of all popular application software programs. In addition, we are committed to providing timely coverage of all program updates and revisions. It is hoped that the consistent STAR Series organization and format will provide a flexible approach to either learning multiple application programs or updating to newer program versions. Please contact your local South-Western/Boyd & Fraser Representative for information on current and future STAR Series offerings.

Introduction to Spreadsheets

What Is a Spreadsheet?

For decades, accountants and other business people have used columnar pads, pencils, and calculators to complete business analyses. These columnar pads helped accountants organize and present their numbers and totals in tables made up of rows and columns. The result of such an analysis is a document called a spreadsheet. These spreadsheets are used in such activities as financial analysis, sales projections, and budgeting. Spreadsheets enable individuals to examine data in a clear, organized, and concise manner.

Figure 1 depicts part of a typical columnar pad sheet used for creating a spreadsheet. The sheet has several columns and a series of rows, both of which are numbered consecutively beginning with the number 1.

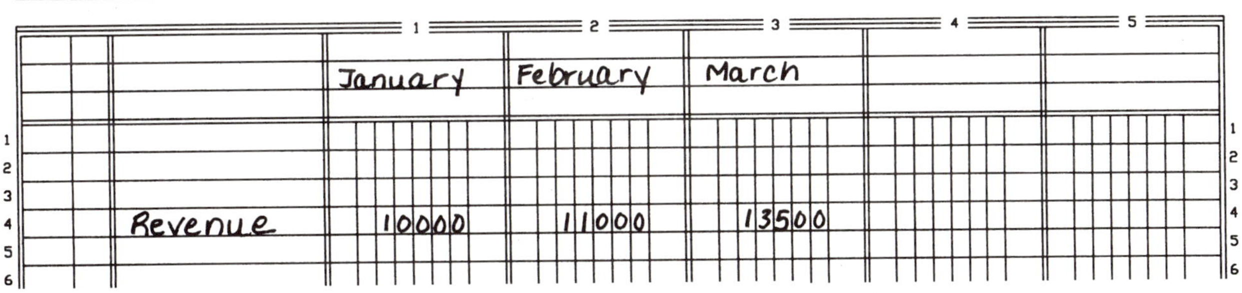

Figure 1 *A Spreadsheet Pad*

A column often represents a time period, for example, a month, a quarter, or a year. The rows typically represent such items as revenue, product quantities, or various types of expenses. For example, in the spreadsheet in Figure 1, the data in the numbered columns is for the months of January, February, and March. The wider unnumbered column to the left of the numbered columns contains entries called labels. Labels identify the items for which entries are placed in the numbered columns. For example, the word "Revenue" in row 4 indicates that the values in this row are the *revenue* amounts for the appropriate months.

In about 1980, electronic spreadsheet software packages became available for personal computers. These programs, such as the popular VisiCalc, automated the process for completing spreadsheets. The programs replaced columnar pads, pencils, and calculators in many business analysis and reporting activities.

Today, more powerful software packages such as Lotus 1-2-3, Microsoft Excel, and Quattro Pro exist. These packages permit the creation of much larger spreadsheets than their predecessors. Not only can you use the software to perform simple calculations, but you can also create formulas using information in the spreadsheet. For example, you can enter Income equals Revenue minus Expenses in your spreadsheet. When you change the value of a given entry in the spreadsheet, for example, Revenue, the software automatically recalculates all formulas impacted by the change and displays the results on your computer screen.

In addition to creating spreadsheets, these software packages can be used to create graphs and to print spreadsheets and graphs. You can also perform some database activities such as sorting and searching for data in the spreadsheet. This book will introduce you to all of these capabilities as implemented by Lotus 1-2-3.

Getting Started

CONCEPTS For many people the answer to the question "What do I do when I turn on my computer?" is "I use Lotus 1-2-3." 1-2-3 turns the almost blank and very limited screen of the operating system into a powerful tool for storing, calculating, and presenting numerically oriented information. This topic shows you how to get into and out of the 1-2-3 program and introduces the 1-2-3 menus.

Starting the Program

10

How you start the 1-2-3 program depends on how your computer has been set up. Check with your instructor or computer support person to find the proper technique for your system. In this book, we assume that you are running 1-2-3 from your hard disk. Make sure the hard disk is the current drive and that the directory containing the 1-2-3 software is the current directory. Then type LOTUS and press the ENTER key to start the program. In a moment you will see the Lotus Access System screen.

TIP You may also start the 1-2-3 program directly by typing 123 at the DOS command prompt and pressing the ENTER key. This method is faster than going through the Lotus Access System and leaves additional memory for your applications.

As its name suggests, the Lotus Access System gives you access to the various 1-2-3 facilities. These facilities are displayed for you across the top of the screen in a list called a **menu**. The three menu options that we are concerned with are 1-2-3, PrintGraph, and Exit. When you enter the Lotus Access System, the 1-2-3 option, which loads the 1-2-3 program, is already highlighted. The PrintGraph option is used to create printed output of 1-2-3 graphs (Topic 16). The Exit option takes you out of 1-2-3 and back to DOS. To select the 1-2-3 option when it is highlighted, you press the ENTER key. After a few moments you will see the 1-2-3 screen. ◀

Understanding the 1-2-3 Screen

The main purpose of the 1-2-3 program is to allow you to manipulate an electronic **worksheet**. Conceptually this worksheet is a grid containing 8192 horizontal rows and 256 vertical columns. The intersection of each row and column defines a **cell**. Each of the more than 2 million cells in the worksheet can store information.

You identify a row by its **row number**, which ranges from 1 through 8192. A column is identified by its **column letter.** Column letters start with A through Z and then become double letter combinations, AA...AZ, BA...BZ, ... IA...IV, for a total of 256 columns. You identify each cell by its **cell address,** formed from its column letter followed by its row number. For example, the cell at the intersection of column D and row 19 has the cell address D19.

Figure 1.1 shows the **1-2-3 screen,** which consists of three sections.

Figure 1.1
The 1-2-3 Screen

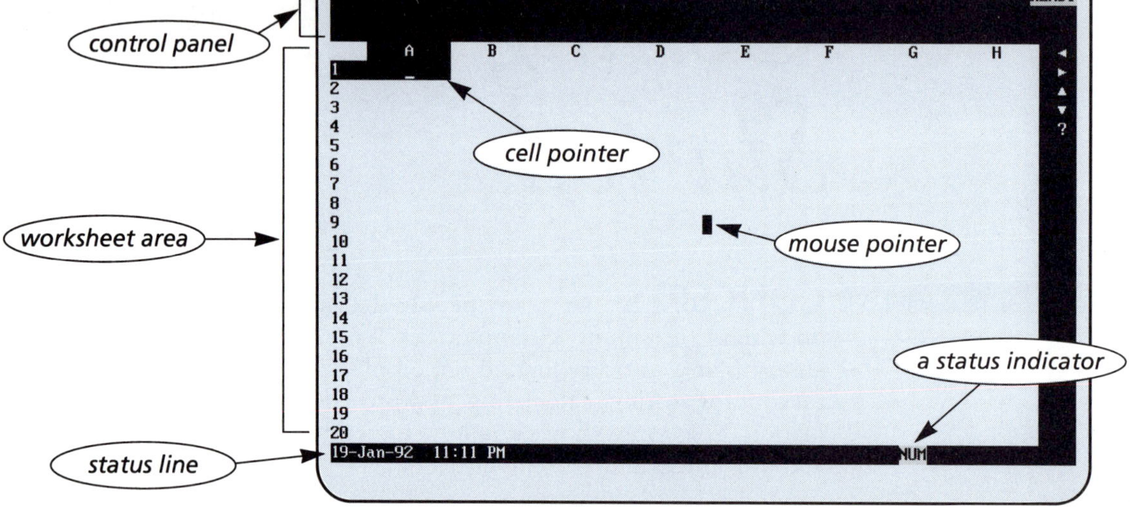

The main portion of the worksheet, called the **worksheet area**, is surrounded by a highlighted border containing column letters across the top and row numbers down the side. This area is where you will be designing and viewing your worksheets. It has the following features:

- The area within the border displays the portion of the 1-2-3 worksheet where you will view the text and numbers you enter into the worksheet as well as the results of the calculations.
- The row numbers and column letters in the border show which of the worksheet columns and rows are currently visible in the worksheet area.
- In the upper left corner of the worksheet area, cell A1 is highlighted. This highlight, called the **cell pointer**, is movable (Topic 2). You use it to select cells in the worksheet and to move the worksheet area to view different portions of the worksheet. The cell containing the highlight is called the **current cell**.

The top three lines of the screen form the **control panel**. As the name suggests, this is where you communicate with 1-2-3 to control its operation. The control panel has the following functions:

- To the left on the first line, 1-2-3 displays the address of the current cell followed by a colon and the **current cell contents**. When you start 1-2-3, this area displays A1: followed by a blank area. This indicates that the cell pointer is in cell A1 and that the cell is currently empty. When the cell contains data, this area is used to display the data in the cell as well as certain cell characteristics.
- To the right on the first line is a highlighted area called the **mode indicator** which tells you what 1-2-3 is doing at the moment. When you start the 1-2-3 program, the mode indicator displays *READY*, indicating that 1-2-3 is ready to process your instructions.

- 1-2-3 uses the second line of the control panel to display its command menus. It also uses this line to prompt you for additional information, to accept your responses, and to collect your input prior to entering it into a cell.
- When the 1-2-3 menus are on the second line of the screen, the third line contains a description of the highlighted menu item or a list of options in the next menu. 1-2-3 also uses this line to display filenames and graph names when appropriate.
- To the right of the worksheet area in the top portion of your screen is the **icon panel**. You select these icons with a mouse.

The bottom line on the screen is called the **status line**. The time and date appear on the left. The rest of the line displays various **status indicators** which tell you when certain keys have been pressed or certain conditions exist. For example, your screen may display the *NUM* indicator showing that the numeric keypad may be used to enter numerical values (Topic 2).

Using Menus with the Keyboard 10

> **TIP**
> Pressing the "less than" key (<) in Ready mode also accesses the command menus.

The major components of any application software program are the information that goes into the program and the commands or tools that the program provides for working with that information. To provide the maximum area for interacting with the worksheet, 1-2-3 keeps its list of commands hidden from view. To access the commands, you press the slash (/) key when you are in Ready mode. The main 1-2-3 menu appears on the second line of the control panel. Simultaneously the mode indicator switches its display to *MENU*. Figure 1.2 displays the Main menu.

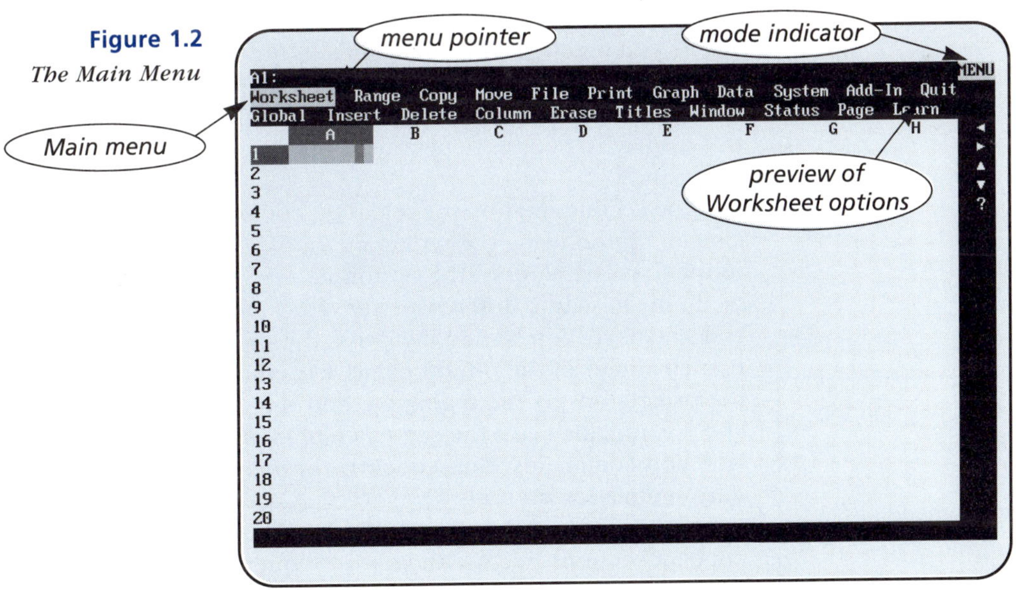

Figure 1.2
The Main Menu

To use a 1-2-3 command, you make a series of selections from successive menus, possibly providing some additional information. When you have made all the selections and provided the information, 1-2-3 carries out the command and then returns to Ready mode.

1-2-3 provides two methods to make selections from menus. When a menu appears in the control panel, it contains a rectangular highlight called the **menu pointer**. The **pointing** method for making menu selections consists of highlighting the desired menu option with the menu pointer and then pressing the ENTER key. The keys used to move the menu pointer are described in Table 1.1.

Table 1.1
Keys Used in 1-2-3 Menus

Keys	Use
/	Activates the 1-2-3 command menu.
→ or SPACEBAR	Moves the menu pointer right one option. If the pointer is highlighting the last option, wraps it around to cover the first option.
←	Moves the menu pointer left one option. If the pointer is on the first option, wraps it around to the last option.
HOME	Moves the pointer to the first option.
END	Moves the pointer to the last option.
↵ENTER	Selects the highlighted option.
ESC	Moves back one level in the command sequence. Returns to Ready mode from the main command menu.
CTRL-BREAK	Cancels the command and returns to Ready mode.

As you highlight the commands in the menu, the third line of the control panel displays a description of the highlighted option or previews the menu that will appear if you select the highlighted command. Examining this display is a convenient way to become familiar with the different 1-2-3 commands.

The second method for selecting commands is called **typing**. To select a menu option using the typing method, you press the key corresponding to the first character of the option name. Since all of the options within a menu begin with a different letter, 1-2-3 recognizes the option you want and selects it. You should not press the ENTER key after you press the first character of the option name. Experienced 1-2-3 users usually make their selections by the typing method since it requires fewer keystrokes and you quickly learn the sequence of characters required to carry out common commands. Consequently, in this book, the tutorials and procedure summaries present the characters necessary to select commands by the typing method. When we talk about commands in the introductory concept sections, we use the entire sequence of command words, for example, the /Worksheet Erase command.

If you make an incorrect selection from a 1-2-3 menu, you can back up one step by pressing the ESCAPE key. To completely cancel your previous selections and return to Ready mode, press the CONTROL-BREAK key combination. ◀

TIP The ESC key and the CTRL-BREAK combination work as long as the command has not been completed. To cancel a command that has been completed, you can use the 1-2-3 Undo feature (Topic 7).

A mouse is a piece of hardware that connects to your computer. If a mouse is connected to your computer, you can use it to select options from a menu.

Move the mouse pointer (usually a reverse-video box) to the control panel. The 1-2-3 Main menu appears on your screen. You can then select a menu option by moving the mouse pointer to a specific option and pressing (or clicking) the mouse button. In this text, the term "mouse button" refers to the left mouse button. You can move back one level in the command structure by pressing the right mouse button (sometimes referred to as the "alternate mouse button").

Accessing DOS

11

Sometimes when you are working with 1-2-3, you will want to access operating system commands or run some other program. For example, you might want to format a diskette or copy files between directories. Rather than ending the 1-2-3 session, you can use the /System command to suspend the 1-2-3 session and work directly with DOS.

When you select /System, the 1-2-3 screen disappears and you are returned to the DOS command prompt. With 1-2-3 temporarily suspended, you can run DOS commands or other programs. However, you should not run any program that will remain in memory after it is completed. Examples of such programs are the DOS PRINT command and various terminate and stay resident (TSR) utilities. When you have finished your DOS activities and are ready to return to 1-2-3, type the word "EXIT" at the DOS command prompt and then press the ENTER key. You are returned to 1-2-3 exactly as you left it.

Ending the 1-2-3 Session

11

To end your 1-2-3 session, you use the /Quit command. To execute this command, you respond to a series of menus.

When you select /Quit, 1-2-3 gives you a menu containing the options No and Yes. This confirming menu allows you to reverse your selection if it was made in error. For example, you may have hit the Q key when you were trying to type a W or an S. Selecting No returns you to Ready mode.

If you select Yes and if you have saved the changes in the worksheet (Topics 3 and 4), the 1-2-3 program ends and returns you to the Lotus Access System. However, if you have modified the worksheet without saving the changes, 1-2-3 provides another menu with the No and Yes options. This time the description line contains a warning that the changes made to the worksheet were not saved. This menu offers additional protection against the loss of unsaved work. Once again selecting No returns you to Ready mode, whereas selecting Yes ends the 1-2-3 program and returns you to the Lotus Access System. Finally, to get back to DOS, you select the Exit option from the Access menu. ◀

TIP

If you started 1-2-3 by typing 123 at the DOS command prompt, the Lotus Access System screen does not appear.

TUTORIAL

In this tutorial, you practice four basic skills: starting 1-2-3, quitting 1-2-3, using 1-2-3 menus, and accessing DOS.

1 Start the 1-2-3 program. To start 1-2-3, you must be in the directory that contains the 1-2-3 program files. The DOS command prompt gives the current directory. Because this book assumes that the 1-2-3 program is on the hard disk drive, the prompt should be similar to C:\123>.

Type	LOTUS	
Press	↵ ENTER	

The Access menu appears at the top of the screen with 1-2-3 highlighted.

Press	↵ ENTER	Selects 1-2-3.

After a brief wait, an empty worksheet is on the screen.

2 Use a menu. Much of the work in building worksheets with 1-2-3 is done by using 1-2-3 commands from the menus. Inputting information into cells by copying from other cells, changing the appearance of the worksheet, and printing out reports are just a few examples of the uses of 1-2-3 menus. Here you practice entering, making selections from, and leaving the 1-2-3 menus.

Press	/	Activates the Main menu. Mode indicator displays *MENU.*

The Main menu appears on the second line of the control panel. Since the Worksheet option is highlighted, the third line contains the worksheet commands.

Press	→	Highlights Range. Range options are on third line of control panel.
Press	↵ ENTER	Selects Range. Range options are on second line of control panel.

You selected Range by pointing. From now on, the keystrokes for selecting from the menu by typing will be given.

Press	ESC	Returns to the Main menu.

The Escape key moves you back a step to the Main menu. The Range option is highlighted.

Press	F	Selects File. File options appear on second line of control panel.
Press	CTRL-BREAK	Exits from the menus. Mode indicator displays *READY*.

Each time you press the Escape key, you move back one level in the menus. You now reenter the menus and then leave by pressing the Escape key repeatedly.

Press	/	Activates the Main menu. Mode indicator displays *MENU*.
Press	W	Selects Worksheet.
Press	C	Selects Column.
Press	ESC three times	Returns to Ready mode.

The mouse can be used to access the 1-2-3 menus and to select an option on any menu. In the next two steps, you are moving the mouse pointer.

Move	mouse pointer to control panel	Activates the Main menu. Mode indicator displays *MENU*.
Move	mouse pointer to a specific menu option	Specifies desired menu option.
Click	mouse button	Selects menu option.
Click	Alternate mouse button twice	Returns to Ready mode.

3 **Access DOS.** If, while working in 1-2-3, you want to use a DOS command such as FORMAT or DIR, you can temporarily leave 1-2-3 and then return directly to what you were doing.

Press	/	Activates the Main menu.
Press	S	Selects System.

The cursor is at the DOS command prompt on the screen. The message "Type EXIT and press ENTER to return to 1-2-3" is on the screen. You now can use whichever DOS commands you want. When you are finished working at the DOS level, you return to what you were doing in 1-2-3.

Type	EXIT	
Press	↵ ENTER	Returns to 1-2-3.

4 **Quit 1-2-3.** When you have finished a 1-2-3 session, you exit 1-2-3 through the Main menu. Usually you should save whatever you have been working on before leaving 1-2-3 (Topic 4).

Press	/	Activates the Main menu.
Press	Q	Selects Quit.
Press	Y	Selects Yes; confirms that you want to leave 1-2-3.

Assuming you have saved the changes you made, 1-2-3 returns to the Access menu. If not, it gives you another No or Yes menu.

Press	E	Selects Exit.

You leave 1-2-3 and return to the DOS command prompt.

PROCEDURE SUMMARY

STARTING THE PROGRAM

Be sure the DOS prompt displays the directory containing the 1-2-3 program.	
At the DOS prompt, type	LOTUS
Enter the input.	↵ ENTER
Select 1-2-3.	↵ ENTER

USING MENUS WITH THE KEYBOARD

Be in Ready mode.	
Activate the Main menu.	/
Select a command by typing its first letter.	(your input)
Return to the prior level of the menus.	ESC
Cancel the command.	CTRL - BREAK

USING MENUS WITH A MOUSE

Be in Ready mode.
Activate the Main menu by moving the mouse pointer to the control panel.

Select a command by moving the mouse pointer to the option and clicking the mouse button.	
Return to the prior level of the menus.	(alternate mouse button)
Cancel the command.	CTRL-BREAK

ACCESSING DOS

Activate the Main menu.	/
Select System.	S
Use the desired DOS commands.	(your input)
End the DOS session by typing	EXIT
Return to the worksheet.	↵ ENTER

ENDING THE 1-2-3 SESSION

Activate the Main menu.	/
Select Quit.	Q
Select Yes.	Y
If you have not saved and still do not wish to save the revisions in your worksheet, select Yes.	Y
Select Exit.	E

EXERCISES

1A Define the following terms:

1. Row number ______
2. Column letter ______
3. Cell ______
4. Cell pointer ______
5. Current cell ______
6. Cell address ______
7. Control panel ______
8. Mode indicator ______
9. Status line ______
10. Worksheet area ______

1B Complete the following tasks:

1. Start the 1-2-3 program by typing "Lotus" and pressing the ENTER key.
2. Exit the 1-2-3 program by using the menu pointer and pressing the ENTER key.
3. Start the 1-2-3 program by typing "123" and pressing the ENTER key.
4. Exit the 1-2-3 program by typing the first letter of the menu options.
5. Start the 1-2-3 program.
6. Access DOS using the Lotus 1-2-3 menus.
7. Format a diskette for later use.
8. Return to 1-2-3.
9. Exit the 1-2-3 program.
10. Activate the Main menu using a mouse.
11. Select the Range option on the Main menu using a mouse.
12. Cancel the command using the CONTROL-BREAK key combination.

Working with 1-2-3

CONCEPTS

Although at any one time the worksheet area displays only a few hundred cells, it is common for a typical application to contain thousands of cells. This topic describes the efficient methods available for moving to these cells, whether or not they happen to be currently visible. You also learn how to use the 1-2-3 Help System, which can instantaneously provide you with interactive help information from anywhere within 1-2-3.

Understanding the Keyboard

You interact with 1-2-3 through your computer keyboard. As seen in Figure 2.1, the keyboard has several sections.

Figure 2.1
The Keyboard

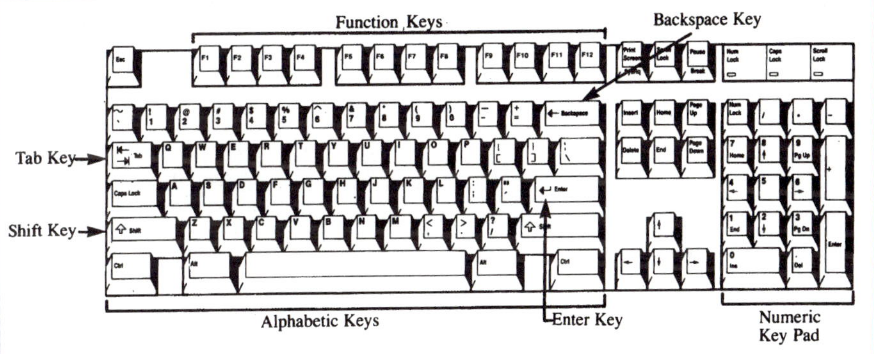

The main part of the keyboard, labeled alphabetic keys in Figure 2.1, contains letters, numbers, and special characters used to type data into the worksheet. Around these keys are other special keys such as the SHIFT key and ENTER key, which have various purposes as described in Table 2.1.

Table 2.1
Special Keys

Name	Key	Function
The following keys are used for data entry and editing.		
BACKSPACE	←BACKSPACE	In editing, erases the character to the left of the cursor.
ENTER	↵ENTER	Signals the completion of an entry or selects an option when pointing.
ESCAPE	ESC	Backs up one step in 1-2-3 commands or erases input data.
DELETE	DELETE	In editing, erases the character above the cursor.
The following keys modify the action of other keys by turning switches on and off.		
CAPS LOCK	CAPS LOCK	Switches letter keys between upper- and lowercase versions.
NUM LOCK	NUM LOCK	Switches the numeric keypad between entering numbers and moving around the worksheet.
SCROLL LOCK	SCROLL LOCK	Switches the arrow keys between moving the cell pointer and moving the worksheet.
The following keys modify the action of other keys when they are held down while another key is pressed.		
ALT	ALT	With other keys, gives them an alternate meaning.
CTRL	CTRL	With the left and right arrow keys, results in more rapid movement.
SHIFT	SHIFT	Gets the uppercase version of a key.

Across the top of the keyboard, or to left of the alphabetic keys on older keyboards, are a series of 10 or 12 **function keys** labeled F1 through F10 or F12. Each of the function keys F1 through F10 performs two special operations in 1-2-3. One operation is obtained when you press the key by itself; the other operation (except for function key F6) is obtained when you press the function key while also holding down the ALT (alternate) key. Table 2.2 describes these keys, which will be treated in this book. 1-2-3 provides a template for you to place next to or around the function keys showing the function key names.

Table 2.2
The 1-2-3 Function Keys

Name	Key	Function	Topic
HELP	F1	Accesses the 1-2-3 Help facility. ◀	2
EDIT	F2	Allows you to edit cell entries or input data.	7
NAME	F3	Displays lists of names such as file and graph names.	4,16
ABSOLUTE	F4	Converts cell references between relative and absolute for copying.	12
GOTO	F5	Allows you to move the cell pointer to a specific cell.	2
WINDOW	F6	Moves the cell pointer between windows.	13
QUERY	F7	Repeats the last data query.	15
GRAPH	F10	Redraws the last graph with current values.	16
UNDO	ALT-F4	Cancels the last change made to the worksheet.	7

TIP The Help facility can also be accessed by moving the mouse pointer to the ? icon in the icon panel and then clicking the mouse button. The icon panel is located to the right of the worksheet area in the top portion of your screen.

To the right of the alphabetic keys is a numeric keypad. In addition to numeric values, the keys on this pad contain arrows and special words such as END and HOME that are associated with moving around the worksheet. On newer keyboards, the numeric keypad is separated from the main keyboard by an area containing the four arrow keys on the bottom and six keys containing the other special terms from the keypad on the top.

The function of the keys in the numeric keypad is determined by the NumLock key. Pressing the NumLock key toggles the *NUM* status indicator on and off in the status line at the bottom of your screen. When the *NUM* indicator is on, the numeric keypad types numbers, decimal points, and so on. When the *NUM* indicator is off, the numeric keypad is used to provide the arrow keys and other functions associated with it. On older keyboards, you should leave the *NUM* indicator off since you will use the numeric keypad in this manner. On newer machines, you have the option of how you wish to use the numeric keypad.

Moving Around the Worksheet

22

It is convenient to think of the worksheet area in the 1-2-3 screen as a movable window that allows you to view a portion of the 1-2-3 worksheet. The area viewed through this window always contains the 1-2-3 cell pointer.

TIP Holding down any of the movement keys causes them to automatically repeat and move the cell pointer rapidly through the worksheet. 1-2-3 may respond more slowly than the keyboard repeats the keys. So, the motion may continue after you take your finger off the key.

The cell pointer has two major functions. First, you use it to identify individual cells to 1-2-3, for example, the cell into which you want to enter data. You select a cell by moving the cell pointer to it. The cell containing the cell pointer is referred to as the **current cell**. The address of the current cell is shown in the upper left corner of the control panel followed by a colon(:) and the current cell contents.

Second, by moving the cell pointer, you may also view different portions of the worksheet. When the cell pointer is moved out of the cells that are visible on the screen, the window given by the worksheet area moves with it. The row and column labels at the edge of the worksheet area change to those of the new section of the worksheet visible on the screen.

You move the cell pointer around the 1-2-3 worksheet using various keys on your keyboard. A table of these **cell pointer-movement keys** is given in Table 2.3. We refer to these keys as the **movement keys** for short. ◀

Table 2.3
The Pointer-Movement Keys

Keys	Use
← ↑ ↓ →	Moves the cell pointer one cell in the indicated direction. ◀
PAGE UP PAGE DOWN	Moves the cell pointer and worksheet area one screen up or down.
CTRL-→ or TAB CTRL-← or SHIFT-TAB	Moves the cell pointer and worksheet area one screen right or left.
HOME	Moves the cell pointer to the upper left corner of the worksheet.
F5, or GOTO	Moves the cell pointer to a user-specified cell.
END-(arrow key)	Moves the cell pointer in the direction of the arrows to the end of a block of data or empty cells.
END-HOME	Moves the cell pointer to the lower right corner of the active worksheet area.

TIP The cell pointer can be moved one cell in the indicated direction by moving the mouse pointer to the appropriate icon (◀,▶,▲,▼) on the icon panel and clicking the mouse button. When you hold down the mouse button with the mouse pointer on a specific icon, the cell pointer continues moving until you take your finger off the mouse button.

The F5 function key, called the **GOTO key**, allows you to move directly to a specific cell. When you press the GOTO (F5) key, 1-2-3 places the message "Enter address to go to: xx" on the second line of the control panel, where xx is the current cell address. Type in the address of the cell you want to go to and press the ENTER key. The cell pointer moves to the cell, adjusting the worksheet area if necessary.

1-2-3 uses the END key to help you move through the worksheet guided by the data contained in the worksheet. Many worksheets have long, continuous blocks of data or empty cells. The END key allows you to move to the beginning or end of such areas. Pressing the END key toggles the *END* status indicator on the status line on and off. Pressing an arrow key when the *END* indicator is on causes a cell pointer that is in the middle of a *continuous* block of cells containing data to move in the direction of the arrow to the last cell in that block. If the cells in the direction of the arrow are empty, the cell pointer moves through them and stops in the first nonempty cell. Pressing the HOME key when the *END* indicator is on moves the cell pointer to the lower right corner of the **active worksheet area**. This is the rectangle starting from cell A1 and bordered on the right and bottom by the last column and row that have contained data.

Using the Help System 23

> **TIP** You can access the Help System by moving the mouse pointer to the ? on the icon panel and clicking the mouse button.

As you are using 1-2-3, you may require assistance to understand a request 1-2-3 is making, to try to discover the appropriate command or calculation to perform, or just to learn more about a new 1-2-3 feature. 1-2-3 provides readily available assistance for all these needs through its **Help System**. You access the Help System using the F1 function key, called the HELP key. When you press this key, 1-2-3 replaces the worksheet area with a **Help screen**. The mode indicator displays *HELP* (Figure 2.2). ◀

Figure 2.2
The Help Screen

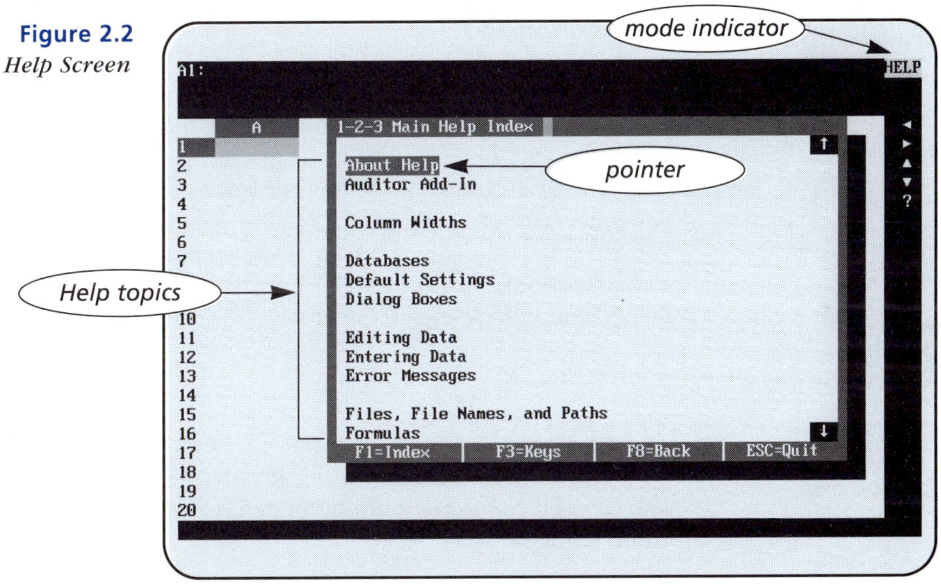

The 1-2-3 help system is **context sensitive**. This means that the Help screen selected is determined by the activity you were involved in when you pressed the HELP (F1) key. Generally 1-2-3 supplies you with a Help screen explaining the steps required to perform that activity.

Within any Help screen you will see additional Help topics either emphasized or in color. One of the topics will be highlighted by a rectangular pointer. To view a Help screen describing any of these topics, highlight the topic and press the ENTER key. Table 2.4 shows the keys that are available in the Help System.

Table 2.4
Keys Used in the Help System

Key	Use
F1 or HELP	Activates the Help System. When in the Help System, returns you to the first Help screen.
← ↑ ↓ →	Moves the pointer over the related Help topics. ◀
HOME	Highlights the first related Help topic.
END	Highlights the last related Help topic.
↵ ENTER	Selects the highlighted Help topic.
←BACKSPACE or F8	Returns to the previous Help screen.
ESC	Leaves the Help System and returns you to 1-2-3.

TIP You can move to various Help topics by moving the mouse pointer to the ↑ or ↓ scroll arrows on the Help screen and clicking the mouse button.

On most Help screens, the last topic is **Help Index**. Selecting the Help Index displays a screen containing topics that describe the major areas of help available in 1-2-3.

1-2-3 remembers the Help screens you chose and the order in which you chose them. Pressing the BACKSPACE key returns you to the previous screen. You use this key if you chose an inappropriate topic or want to view a series of related topics from a previous screen. Each time you press the BACKSPACE key, 1-2-3 moves back one screen. Pressing the HELP (F1) key when you are in the Help System returns you to the first screen. When you are finished using the Help System, press the ESCAPE key or click the alternate mouse button to return to what you were doing in 1-2-3. Everything will be exactly as it was prior to pressing the HELP key.

TUTORIAL

In this tutorial, you practice moving the cell pointer around the worksheet and using the Help System. As you begin the tutorial, the cell pointer should be in cell A1, which is where it is when you enter 1-2-3.

1 **Move a cell at a time.** You start by moving the cell pointer around the worksheet one cell at a time.

Press	→	Moves cell pointer right to cell B1.

The cell address on the first line in the control panel changes to B1.

Press	↓	Moves cell pointer down to cell B2.

> **TIP** You can move one cell to the left, right, up, or down by moving the mouse pointer to the ◄, ►, ▲, or ▼ icon, respectively, and clicking the mouse button.

Press	←	Moves cell pointer left to cell A2. ◄
Press	↑	Moves cell pointer up to cell A1.
Press	↑	Cell pointer does not move.

The system beeps to alert you that the cell pointer could not move since there is no cell above cell A1.

Press	→ seven times	Moves cell pointer to cell H1 on right edge of screen.
Press	→	Moves cell pointer right one cell.

The worksheet area now displays a different portion of the worksheet area. Column I appears on the right edge of the worksheet area. Column A disappears from the worksheet area. The cell pointer is in cell I1. You now return the cell pointer directly to cell A1.

Press	HOME	Moves cell pointer to cell A1.

2 **Move a screen at a time.** You now move around the worksheet area one screen at a time.

Press	CTRL-→	Moves worksheet area and cell pointer right one screen.

The cell pointer is in cell I1. The screen displays cells I1 to P20 reading from the upper left to the lower right.

Press	PAGE DOWN	Moves worksheet area down one screen.

The cell pointer is in cell I21. The screen displays cells I21 through P40.

Press	CTRL-←	Moves worksheet area left one screen.

The cell pointer is in cell A21. The screen displays cells A21 through H40.

Press	PAGE UP	Moves worksheet area up one screen.

> **TIP** You can move a screen right or left by using the TAB key. Pressing the TAB key alone moves the cell pointer a screen to the right. Pressing the TAB key with the SHIFT key moves the cell pointer a screen to the left.

The cell pointer is back in cell A1. The screen displays cells A1 through H20. There is an alternate way to move right and left one screen at a time. ◄

3 **Move using GOTO and END.** If you want to go directly to a specific cell, particularly to one that is far from the current cell, use the GOTO (F5) key.

Press	F5	Activates GOTO. Mode indicator displays *POINT*.

The message "Enter address to go to: A1" is in the second line of the control panel, where A1 is the current cell. You type the address of your destination, and it replaces A1 as the prompt response.

Type	D5	Specifies cell D5 as destination.

D5 replaces A1 as the response to the prompt in the control panel. The "D" need not be capitalized.

Press	↵ ENTER	Moves cell pointer to cell D5.
Press	F5	
Type	CD100	Specifies cell CD100 as destination.
Press	↵ ENTER	Moves cell pointer to cell CD100.

TIP The usefulness of moving through the worksheet using the End key together with an arrow key will be made clearer in later topics when some cells in the worksheet are filled.

With cell D5 in the middle of the worksheet area, the cell pointer moved to it. Since cell CD100 was not on the screen when GOTO was activated, it is now in the upper left corner of the worksheet area.

Press	HOME	Moves cell pointer to cell A1.

You can use the End key together with an arrow key to move instantly through a row or column of nonempty (or empty) cells. ◀

Press	END	Turns on *END* indicator on status line.
Press	↓	Moves cell pointer to cell A8192.

The cell pointer moves directly to the bottom of column A since the rest of the cells in column A are empty. The *END* indicator on the status line is off. To use the feature again, you must press the End key again.

Press	END	Turns on *END* indicator.
Press	→	Moves cell pointer to cell IV8192; turns off *END* indicator.
Press	HOME	Returns to cell A1.

4 **Use the Help System.** You can access the Help System at any time in 1-2-3. In this section, you access the Help System, practice selecting topics from the screens, and leave the system. To demonstrate the context-sensitive nature of the Help screens, you start by activating GOTO.

Press	F5	
Press	F1	Displays Help screen for GOTO. Mode indicator displays *HELP*.

TIP You can access the Help Index by moving the mouse pointer to the "F1=Index" phrase and clicking the mouse button.

The phrase "F1=Index" is always on a Help screen, so you can easily access the index if the material on the screen is not relevant to your question(s). Here the phrase appears in the lower left corner of the screen. To access the Help Index, press the F1 key. You bring up the screens on the topics you want by highlighting the appropriate phrase and pressing the Enter key. ◀

Press	F1	Brings the Help Index to the screen.
Press	↓ nine times	Highlights "/File."
Press	↵ENTER	Displays Help screen on File options.

You now return to the previous screens and then move forward again.

Press	←BACKSPACE	Returns Help Index to the screen.
Press	←BACKSPACE	Returns to screen on the GOTO (F5) function key.
Press	F1	Returns Help Index to the screen.

Each time you press the Backspace key, you return to the previous screen.

Press	(↓) two times	Highlights "Column Widths."
Press	(↵ ENTER)	Displays Help screen on "Column Widths."
Press	(F1)	Returns you to Help Index.
Press	(ESC)	Leaves Help System.

You return to exactly where you were when you entered the Help System. In this case, you have the GOTO message on the control panel waiting for your response.

Press	(ESC)	Returns to Ready mode.

PROCEDURE SUMMARY

MOVING AROUND THE WORKSHEET

To move one cell at a time using the pointer-movement keys:

Move horizontally.	(→) or (←)
Move vertically.	(↑) or (↓)

To move one screen at a time:

Move horizontally.	(CTRL)-(→) or (CTRL)-(←)
Move vertically.	(PAGE DOWN) or (PAGE UP)

To move to the top left corner of the worksheet:

Press	(HOME)

To move to a specified cell:

Activate GOTO.	(F5)
Type the cell address of the destination.	(your input)
Enter the input.	(↵ ENTER)

To move to the filled cell at the next boundary of empty and filled cells in a column or row:

Activate END.	(END)
Move in the desired direction.	(arrow key)

MOVING AROUND THE WORKSHEET USING A MOUSE

To move horizontally one cell at a time:

Move the mouse pointer to the ▶ or ◀ icon.

Click the mouse button.

To move vertically one cell at a time:

Move the mouse pointer to the ▼ or ▲ icon.

Click the mouse button.

USING THE HELP SYSTEM

Enter the Help System.	F1
Select a Help topic from the current screen.	
Highlight your choice.	(arrow keys)
Display the new screen.	↵ ENTER
Return to the previous screen.	← BACKSPACE
Return to the initial screen.	F1
Leave the Help System and return to the worksheet.	ESC

EXERCISES

2A Complete the following tasks:

1. If the cell pointer is not in cell A1, press the HOME key.
2. Use the RIGHT ARROW key to move the cell pointer to cell M1.
3. Use the LEFT ARROW key to move the cell pointer to cell A1.
4. Use the DOWN ARROW key to move the cell pointer to cell A32.
5. Use the UP ARROW key to move the cell pointer to cell A1.
6. Use the PAGE DOWN key to move the cell pointer to cell A121.
7. Use the PAGE UP key to move the cell pointer to cell A1.
8. Use the CONTROL-RIGHT ARROW keys to move the cell pointer to cell Q1.
9. Use the CONTROL-LEFT ARROW keys to move the cell pointer to cell A1.

10. Use the F5 key to move the cell pointer to cell AZ4190.
11. Use the HOME key to move the cell pointer to cell A1.
12. Use the TAB key to move the cell pointer to cell Q1.
13. Use the SHIFT-TAB keys to move the cell pointer to cell A1.
14. Use the arrow keys to move the cell pointer to cell D8.
15. Use the arrow keys to move the cell pointer to cell A1.
16. Use a mouse to move the cell pointer to cell I1.
17. Use a mouse to move the cell pointer to cell D10.
18. Use a mouse to move the cell pointer to cell A1.

2B Complete the following tasks:

1. Press the F1 key to access the Help System.
2. Examine what is said about the F1 key in the function key section of the Help System.
3. Exit the Help System.
4. Use a mouse to access the Help System.
5. Examine what is said about Mouse Basics.
6. Exit the Help System.

TOPIC 3

Entering Data

CONCEPTS This topic discusses the types of data that may be stored in the 1-2-3 worksheet and how to enter this data from the keyboard. The 1-2-3 worksheet consists of over two million cells, any of which may be used to store data. What data you put in these cells, and where you put it, defines your application.

1-2-3 distinguishes two different types of data: labels and values. **Labels** contain textual information (such as report headings, row or column names, and comments) that describes the contents of the worksheet or provides other written details. **Values** contain numerical information that can either be input directly as numbers or computed from formulas.

Using the keyboard to make an entry into a cell is a three-step process.

1. While in Ready mode, you place the cell pointer in the cell in which you want the data entered.
2. You type the entry at the keyboard. As you type, the characters appear on the second line of the control panel.
3. You enter what you have typed into the cell either by pressing the ENTER key or by moving from the cell using any of the movement keys.

Entering Labels 35

When you type the first character of your entry, 1-2-3 examines the character to determine whether you are entering a label or a value. If the initial character is a numeral or one of the numeric symbols that 1-2-3 associates with numbers or formulas (that is, + – @ (. # or $), 1-2-3 assumes you are entering a value and displays *VALUE* in the mode indicator. Any other character signals the entry of a label. In this case, the mode indicator displays *LABEL*.

Based on this rule, 1-2-3 would interpret entries such as "1995 REVENUE", "43 Main Street", and "(203)-555-1212" as values when, in fact, they are intended to be labels. To indicate that such an entry is a label, you must precede it with one of the **label prefixes** shown in Table 3.1.

Table 3.1
Label Prefixes

Prefix	Use
'	Aligns a label to the left in a cell.
"	Aligns a label to the right in a cell.
^	Aligns a label in the center of a cell.
\	Repeats the characters following it to fill the cell.
¦	Indicates a label that is not to be printed or one that contains instructions for the printer.

Labels can contain up to 240 characters. However, most are much shorter. When a label is shorter than the width of its cell, the alignment of the label in the cell becomes important. You control the alignment by preceding the text of the label with one of three label alignment prefixes: the apostrophe ('), the quotation mark ("), and the caret (^). As shown in Table 3.1, these prefixes produce left alignment, right alignment, and centering of the label in the cell, respectively.

1-2-3 requires that any label that has been stored in a cell begin with some label prefix. If you have typed a label that does not already begin with one of the prefixes in Table 3.1, 1-2-3 automatically inserts an apostrophe in front of the label before storing it in the cell. In the worksheet area, the label is left aligned and displayed with its first character at the left edge of the cell. The remainder of the cell after the last character is left blank. Note that the worksheet area displays only the text following the label prefix. The label prefix determines the positioning of the text in the cell, but the prefix itself is not visible. You can view the label prefix by moving to the cell containing the label and examining the current cell contents in the upper left corner of the control panel.

> **TIP** The blank placed to the right of right-aligned labels makes their alignment consistent with the way 1-2-3 displays numerical values (next section and Topic 10). As a result, you will frequently use right-aligned labels as the headings of columns containing numerical data.

To right align or center a label in a cell, you must type the quotation mark or caret, respectively, as the first character in the label. The prefix is then followed by the label text. Right-aligned labels display with a single space between the last character in the label and the right edge of the cell. ◀

A label that is longer than the width of its cell is called a **long label**. In displaying long labels, 1-2-3 places the first character of the label at the left edge of the cell containing the label. The subsequent characters fill the cell and flow over into adjacent empty cells to the right. The label continues to the right until all characters are shown or until it encounters a cell containing data. In the latter case, the display is truncated at the left edge of the nonempty cell. Because the characters of a long label flow over into adjacent empty cells, you might think that these cells contain those portions of the label as data. However, if you move to these cells and view the current cell contents in the control panel, you can see that the cells are empty. Similarly, if the display of a long label is truncated by a nonempty cell, the cell entry itself is not truncated. You can also see this by viewing the current cell contents of the cell containing the label. The rest of the label could be displayed by widening columns (Topic 10) or by erasing the contents of the nonempty cell (Topic 7).

The backslash (\), called the repeating label prefix, causes the characters that follow it to be duplicated to fill the entire cell. Combinations such as \- or \= fill the entire cell with a single or double line of dashes, respectively. These lines are often used to show column totals, to divide sections of the worksheet, or to provide emphasis.

The split vertical bar (¦) can be used to indicate a label that is to appear in the worksheet area but is not to be printed in reports. The prefix also identifies text information that controls the printer (Topic 14).

Entering Numbers

(36)

> **TIP** Do not precede numerical values with a quotation mark or any other alignment character because 1-2-3 regards the input as a label. 1-2-3 treats all labels as if they had a numerical value of zero.

Numbers are entered either from the top row of the alphabetic keys or, if the *NUM* indicator is on, from the numeric keypad. Indicate negative numbers by typing a minus sign as the first character. Indicate decimal digits by preceding them with a period. If the decimal point is the first character in your entry, 1-2-3 adds a leading zero when the entry is stored in the cell. Commas may not be used when entering numbers.

Numbers always display right aligned in a cell. As it does with right-aligned labels, 1-2-3 leaves a single space between the last digit displayed and the right edge of the cell. This allows the use of parentheses to indicate negative values and of percent symbols to indicate percentages (Topic 10). ◀

Correcting Errors

(36)

Errors are a major consideration in creating and using spreadsheets. Most realistic applications have hundreds if not thousands of cells containing formulas, numerical data, and text. For these worksheets to be totally correct requires an extremely high level of accuracy. You achieve this accuracy by adequately planning your worksheet ahead of time, by developing your worksheets using methods that minimize typographical or other input errors, and by thoroughly testing your worksheets after they are created.

1-2-3 provides two simple methods for correcting typing errors that you detect prior to storing your entry in the cell. First, pressing the BACKSPACE key one or more times erases the characters at the end of the entry on the second line of the control panel. You may then resume typing. Second, pressing the ESCAPE key cancels the entire entry and returns you to Ready mode. You can then begin retyping the entry.

1-2-3 itself can detect errors. Although 1-2-3 accepts any input for a label, it only accepts values that are properly formed. For example, if you type 1,000 as your entry, 1-2-3 indicates that you are entering a value since the first character is a numeral. However, when you try to store the entry, 1-2-3 does not accept it because values cannot contain commas. You will hear a beep and 1-2-3 will change the mode indicator to *EDIT*. Topic 7 discusses how you can use the 1-2-3 editing facilities to correct your entry. For the time being, you can either use the BACKSPACE key to make corrections and then press the ENTER key to store your entry, or you can press the ESCAPE key twice to get back to Ready mode. (The first time you press ESCAPE, the entire entry is erased. The second time you press it, the mode indicator changes to *READY*.) This type of error occurs frequently when you are entering a label that begins with a number and you have forgotten to include the leading label prefix.

If incorrect data has been entered into a cell, you may correct it by simply entering the correct data into the cell. The new cell entry replaces the original contents. In addition there are techniques for erasing data from cells and for editing existing entries without totally retyping them (Topic 7).

TUTORIAL

In this tutorial, you build a simple worksheet containing labels and numbers. The basic worksheet constructed in this tutorial will be used and modified in most of the later tutorials. As part of this building process, you will make some deliberate mistakes, which you then correct. Use the same techniques to correct any *unintentional* mistakes you make. To begin the tutorial, you should first start the 1-2-3 program. An empty worksheet with the cell pointer in cell A1 appears on the screen.

1 **Enter a label.** You start by entering a label for the heading of the first column. All letters are to be entered as capitals.

Press	CAPS LOCK	Turns on *CAPS* indicator on status line.
Type	P	

TIP To enter information using a mouse, type the label or number. Then move the mouse pointer to the control panel and click the mouse button.

The mode indicator displays *LABEL* since the first keystroke is a letter. A "P" is on the second line of the control panel.

Type	RODUCT	Displays PRODUCT on second line of control panel.
Press	↵ ENTER	Enters PRODUCT in cell A1; mode indicator displays *READY*. ◄

Note that, by default, the label is left aligned in the cell. The current cell contents in the control panel contain 'PRODUCT. 1-2-3 has automatically supplied the apostrophe, the left alignment prefix. The apostrophe is not visible in the worksheet area.

Press	↓ twice	Moves cell pointer to cell A3.

2 **Correct mistakes.** You now start to enter the product names down the first column. In the process of entering the first two names, you will deliberately make some errors. These mistakes are corrected in one of three ways:

1. Replacing incorrect cell entries with correct cell entries.
2. Using the Escape key to cancel the information from the control panel rather than entering it into the cell.
3. Using the Backspace key to erase typing errors.

Type	NAIL	Displays NAIL on control panel.
Press	↵ENTER	Enters NAIL into cell A3.

You want to change the entry in cell A3. You simply enter the new contents, which replace the old contents.

Type	NAILS	Displays NAILS on control panel.
Press	↵ENTER	Replaces NAIL with NAILS as cell A3 entry.
Press	↓	Moves cell pointer to cell A4.
Type	CREWS	

You recognize the typing error. Since this name is incorrect, you do not want to enter it into the worksheet.

Press	ESC	Returns to *READY* mode; enters nothing into cell A4.
Type	SCREWD	

Again you recognize the typing error. Here it is easier to correct the error than to retype the entire entry.

TIP: To enter data into the current cell and move to the next cell, type the data and move the mouse pointer to an appropriate icon on the icon panel. Then click the mouse button.

Press	←BACKSPACE	Erases "D" at end of word.
Type	S	Adds an "S" at end of word.
Press	↵ENTER	Enters SCREWS into cell A4.

3 **Enter a column of labels.** You now enter the rest of the product names, which are labels. You use the arrow keys, which both enter the data into the current cell *and* move you to the next cell. If you make any typing errors, use the previous techniques to correct them. ◀

Press	↓	Moves cell pointer to cell A5.
Type	BOLTS	
Press	↓	Enters BOLTS into cell A5; moves cell pointer to cell A6.
Type	NUTS	
Press	↓	Enters NUTS into cell A6; moves cell pointer to cell A7.
Type	WASHERS	

Press	↓ twice	Enters WASHERS into cell A7; moves cell pointer to cell A9.
Type	TOTAL	
Press	→	Enters TOTAL; moves cell pointer to cell B9.

You now move to the top of the second column to enter the heading for the second column.

Press	END	Turns on *END* indicator on status line.
Press	↑	Moves cell pointer to cell B1.

The End key followed by the Up Arrow moves the cell pointer through the column of empty cells to the top of the worksheet column.

Type	REVENUE	
Press	↵ENTER	Enters REVENUE.

Your screen should look like Figure 3.1.

Figure 3.1
Revenue: Labels

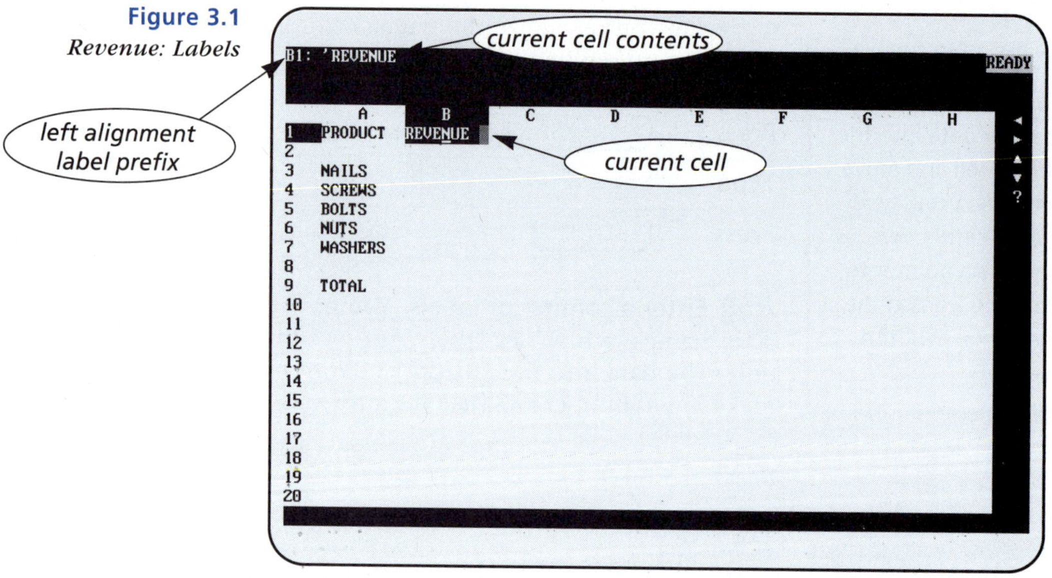

4 **Enter numbers.** In the second column, you enter the revenue data for the products. The revenue data are numbers.

Press	↓ twice	Moves cell pointer to cell B3.
Type	2	

The mode indicator displays *VALUE* since the first keystroke is a number. A "2" is on the second line of the control panel.

Type	25	
Press	↵ ENTER	Enters 225 into cell B3; mode indicator displays *READY*.

225, the revenue value, is right aligned because values are automatically right aligned.

Press	↓	Moves cell pointer to B4.
Type	350	
Press	↓	Enters 350; moves cell pointer to cell B5.
Type	300	
Press	↓	Enters 300; moves cell pointer to cell B6.
Type	250	
Press	↓	Enters 250; moves cell pointer to cell B7.
Type	200	
Press	↓ twice	Enters 200; moves cell pointer to cell B9.
Type	1325	This is the sum of the product revenues.
Press	↵ ENTER	Enters 1325 in cell B9.

Here you have entered the sum of the product revenues as a number. In Topic 6, you learn how to enter a formula so that the computer will do the computation and automatically adjust the sum whenever changes are made to any of the revenue numbers. Your screen should look like Figure 3.2.

Figure 3.2
Revenue: Numbers

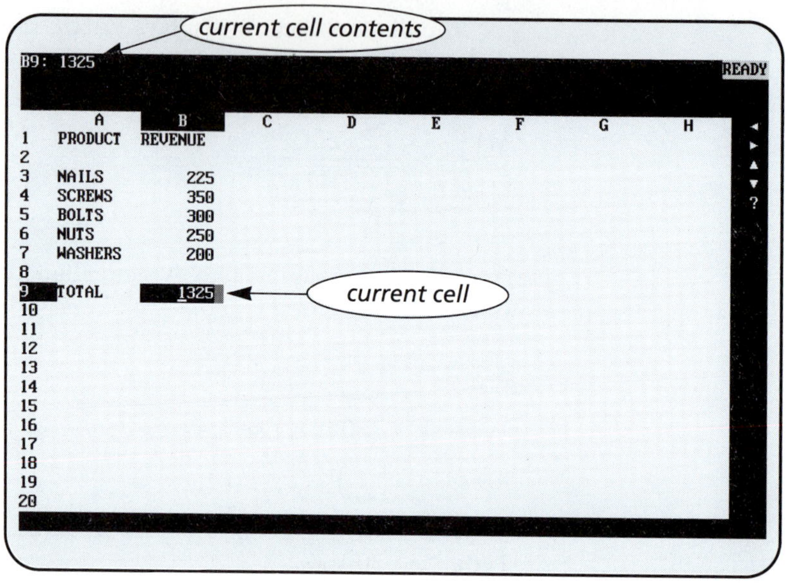

5 **Use label prefixes.** The column heading and the column entries are not aligned. The heading, as a label, is left aligned, and the data, as numbers, are right aligned. You reenter the column heading right aligned over the column entries.

Press	↑ twice	
Press	END, ↑	Uses the End key to move.
Press	↑ twice	Moves cell pointer to cell B1.
Type	"	

The mode indicator displays *LABEL*. Typing a " first right aligns the label.

Type	REVENUE	
Press	↵ ENTER	Enters REVENUE into cell B1 right aligned.

You move to A9 using the GOTO key to change TOTAL from left aligned to centered.

Press	F5	Displays "Enter address to go to: B1" on control panel.
Type	A9	Specifies A9 as cell address of destination.

A9 replaces B1 as the response to the prompt "Enter the address to go to:".

Press	↵ ENTER	Moves cell pointer to cell A9.
Type	^	Centers the label.
Type	TOTAL	
Press	↵ ENTER	Replaces left-aligned TOTAL with centered TOTAL.

6 **Enter underlining, long labels, and numbers as labels.** You finish the worksheet by entering some underlining and footnotes. First, you underline the column headings with a single underline using the backslash (\) and the dash (-). Using the backslash fills the cell with underlining and, if used in adjacent cells, gives the appearance of a continuous line.

Press	F5	Activates GOTO feature.
Type	A2	Specifies cell A2 as destination.
Press	↵ ENTER	Moves cell pointer to cell A2.
Type	\–	
Press	→	Fills cell A2 with underlining; moves cell pointer to cell B2.

If the backslash is the first keystroke in a cell, the cell is filled with the characters that follow. Here the dash provides the underlining.

Type	\–	
Press	END, ↓	Fills cell B2 with underlining; moves cell pointer to cell B7.

The End key followed by the Down Arrow moves the cell pointer through the column of filled cells to the last filled cell.

Press	↓	Moves cell pointer to cell B8.

You separate the column of revenue values from the total of these values with a partial underlining right aligned.

Type	"-----	
Press	↵ ENTER	Partially underlines column with 5 right-aligned dashes.

You move to cell A16 to leave space for additional data to be added later. You enter double underlining with the backslash and the equal sign to separate the body of the worksheet from the footnotes.

Press	F5	
Type	A16	
Press	↵ ENTER	Moves cell pointer to cell A16.
Type	\=	
Press	→	Fills cell A16 with double underlining; moves cell pointer to cell B16.
Type	\=	
Press	↓	Fills cell B16 with double underlining; moves cell pointer to cell B17.
Press	←	Moves cell pointer to cell A17.
Press	CAPS LOCK	Turns off *CAPS* indicator on status line.
Type	Prepared by Roger Jones	
Press	↓	Enters phrase into cell A17; moves cell pointer to cell A18.

On the screen the phrase in cell A17 appears to use cell B17 and part of cell C17. In fact these cells are empty. A long label displays across as much screen space as is available to it.

Type	11/17/91	Mode indicator displays *VALUE.*
Press	↵ ENTER	Enters 0.007110 in cell A18.

You have attempted to enter a date. 1-2-3 treats the entry as a value because the first keystroke was a number. 1-2-3 does the indicated division, displaying the result of the computation in cell A18. You replace the value with the date as a left-aligned label.

Type	'11/17/91	Mode indicator displays *LABEL*.
Press	↵ ENTER	Enters the date as a label.

You have entered a simple worksheet. It should look like the one in Figure 3.3.

Figure 3.3
Completed Revenue Worksheet

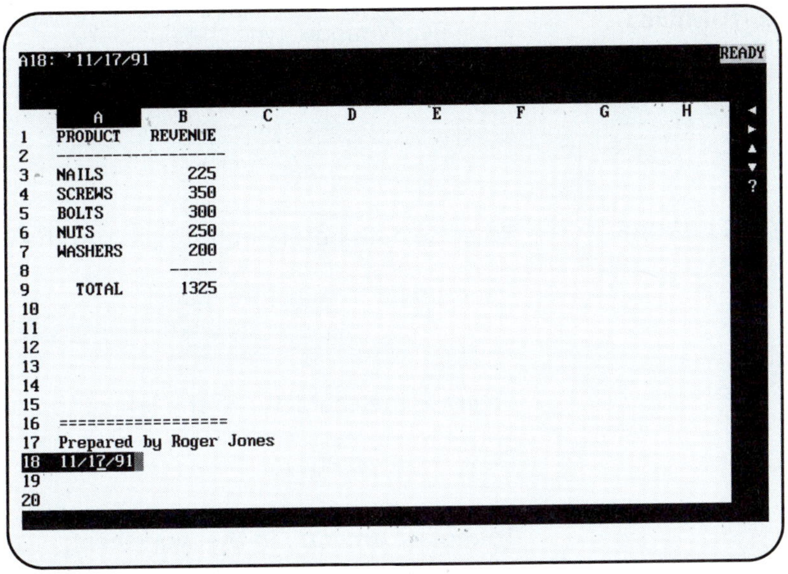

You now have three choices. First, you can end the 1-2-3 session using the Quit command. In that case, this worksheet is lost and you must re-create it at the beginning of the next tutorial. Second, you can look at section 2 of the tutorial in Topic 4 to see how to save this worksheet as a file on your data disk. Third, you can continue to work through the tutorial in Topic 4 where you will, as part of learning how to save and retrieve files, save this worksheet.

PROCEDURE SUMMARY

ENTERING LABELS

To enter a label in the current cell:

Make sure the label begins with a letter or an appropriate label prefix.	
From Ready mode, type the label.	(your input)
Enter the input.	↵ENTER or (pointer-movement keys or mouse)

To fill the current cell with specified character(s):

From Ready mode, type the repeating label prefix.	\
Type the desired character(s).	(your input)
Enter the input.	↵ENTER or (pointer-movement keys or mouse)

ENTERING NUMBERS

From Ready mode, type the number.	(your input)
Enter the input.	↵ENTER or (pointer-movement keys or mouse)

CORRECTING ERRORS

To erase data before entering it into the worksheet:

Cancel data from control panel.	ESC or click alternate mouse button

To erase the character to the left of the cursor:

Erase a character.	←BACKSPACE

To replace an entry in the worksheet:

Move the cell pointer to the cell to be changed.	(pointer-movement keys or mouse)
Type the new data.	(your input)
Enter the input.	↵ENTER

EXERCISES

3A Enter the following labels and numbers in a worksheet:

1. Enter your name in cell A1.
2. Enter the current date in cell A2. Be sure to put the month name first.
3. Enter the text "Proxuct" in cell A4.
4. Correct the label in cell A4 so it appears as "Product".
5. Right align the text "Units" in cell B4.
6. Enter the text "Tires" in cell A5.
7. Enter the number 697 in cell B5.
8. Enter the text "Batteries" in cell A6.
9. Enter the number 178 in cell B6.
10. Change the number in cell B5 to 865.
11. Exit the 1-2-3 program.

3B Enter the following labels and numbers in a worksheet:

1. Enter the text "Able Company" in cell A1.
2. Enter the text "Product" in cell A2.
3. Enter the text "Washers" in cell A3.
4. Enter the text "Dryers" in cell A4.
5. Center the text "Q1," which means Quarter 1, in cell B2.
6. Enter the numbers 1000 in cell B3 and 2300 in cell B4.
7. Exit the 1-2-3 program.

Saving, Retrieving, and Erasing Worksheets

CONCEPTS

1-2-3 calls the worksheet that you see on your screen the **current worksheet**. It stores the information for this worksheet in the main memory (RAM) of your computer. Turning off your computer, quitting 1-2-3, or erasing the current worksheet to start a new one destroys this information.

To retain your worksheets between sessions, 1-2-3 uses special files called **worksheet files**. These files contain all the information present in a current worksheet. You transfer information to and from worksheet files, and manage these files, through the 1-2-3 File commands.

> **TIP** The directory that 1-2-3 initially assigns as the current directory is called the **default directory**. If the default directory is not A:\, you can use the /Worksheet Global Default Directory command to change it to A:\, followed by the /Worksheet Global Default Update command to make the change permanent.

Specifying Where to Store Files

46

Worksheet files stored on disks, particularly on a hard disk, are frequently organized by placing them in different directories. For example, budgeting files might be kept in one directory and marketing files in another one. In practice, you normally work with only one of these directories at a time. When you start your session, 1-2-3 has established some directory as the **current directory**. Unless instructed otherwise, 1-2-3 assumes that all file commands apply to the files in this directory. In this book, the assumption is that the current directory is A:\, the root directory on the A drive. ◀

You change the current directory through the /File Directory command. When you select the /File Directory command, 1-2-3 displays the current directory and asks you for a new directory. If you want to retain the current value, just press ENTER. (This is a convenient way to view the current directory setting.) Otherwise, you type in the desired directory and press ENTER. Your entry may contain both the disk drive and the path to any directory on the disk drive. C:\123 refers to the path to the LOTUS subdirectory on the hard disk.

Saving a Worksheet to a File

47

> **TIP** To use a different directory, you must first press ESC twice and then type in the path to the desired directory, followed by the filename.

To save the current worksheet as a worksheet file, you use the /File Save command. You must specify a name for the file. The first time you save a worksheet, 1-2-3 provides a list of the worksheet files that are present in the current directory. You may select one of these filenames, but doing so replaces the worksheet stored in that file with the current worksheet. Therefore you should normally use a new name. As you begin typing the filename, 1-2-3 inserts it after the path to the current directory in the control panel. As a result, 1-2-3 automatically creates the worksheet file in the current directory. ◀

Filenames for worksheet files follow the normal DOS rules. They consist of up to eight letters, numbers, or some special characters, but they may not contain spaces. The name should reflect the contents of the worksheet. 1-2-3 automatically assigns an extension of .WK1 to the file to distinguish worksheet files from other files on your disk.

As long as the filename you supply does not duplicate the name of an existing file, 1-2-3 creates a worksheet file with the name you specified and copies the contents of the current worksheet from main memory into the file. The current worksheet is left unchanged, and you can continue to work with it.

Since any further changes you make to the worksheet in memory do not automatically change the worksheet file on disk, it is a good idea to save your worksheet to a disk frequently. Then if your computer loses power or you make a mistake that damages the worksheet in memory, you can retrieve the previously saved version of the worksheet from the disk, without losing too much work.

> **TIP** You can use the /Worksheet Global Default Other Clock command to change the left corner of the status line to display the name of the file associated with the current worksheet.

To facilitate this saving process, 1-2-3 remembers the name you gave the worksheet when you last saved it. The next time you use the /File Save command, 1-2-3 suggests using the previous filename for the updated worksheet. Pressing the ENTER key accepts this suggestion. Alternatively, to leave the contents of the previous worksheet file undisturbed, you can type in a new filename. Thus, for example, you could develop a series of worksheet files called PLAN1, PLAN2, and so on by changing the contents of the current worksheet to incorporate different plan assumptions and saving the worksheet with a different filename after entering each set of assumptions. ◀

Whenever you try to save a worksheet using a filename that is already in use, 1-2-3 issues a warning in the form of a menu that offers three options. The Cancel option leaves the original worksheet file and the current worksheet unchanged. The Replace option saves the current worksheet by replacing the previous worksheet file with a new one containing the current worksheet. The Backup option creates a backup copy of the previous worksheet file and then saves the current worksheet with the filename you selected. The backup copy has the same root filename with the extension .BAK.

Erasing the Worksheet from Main Memory

47

To begin a new worksheet when the current worksheet contains information, you must first erase the current worksheet from main memory. You do this with the /Worksheet Erase command.

If you want to retain the contents of the current worksheet, you must save it to a file prior to executing the /Worksheet Erase command. For added protection against losing valuable data, the /Worksheet Erase command provides a final menu with No or Yes options. This gives you a chance to reconsider your decision. Select No to keep the current worksheet unchanged. If you select Yes, 1-2-3 erases the current worksheet from main memory and places you in an empty worksheet exactly as though you had just started the 1-2-3 program. Note that the /Worksheet Erase command itself does not change any information on disk.

Retrieving a Worksheet

47

You store your worksheets in worksheet files because you expect to use and change them later. For example, you may want to access an old worksheet to add data for the current month, to try out new assumptions in a model, or to restructure the worksheet to change the output reports. To work with a worksheet that you previously saved to a worksheet file, you use the /File Retrieve command. This command first erases the current worksheet, then copies the data stored in the worksheet file into main memory, and finally displays the worksheet on the screen after erasing the current worksheet. The retrieved worksheet appears exactly as it was when you saved it. The cell pointer is even in the same position. Since the /File Retrieve command erases the current worksheet, you should be sure to save it prior to retrieving the new one.

When you select the /File Retrieve command, 1-2-3 requests the name of the file you want to retrieve. Simultaneously, on the third line of the control panel, 1-2-3 displays a partial list of the worksheet files in the current directory. If you know the name of the file you want, you can type it at this point and then press ENTER. It is not necessary to supply the filename extension.

Alternatively you may select the file by searching for and highlighting the filename in the list of files. Table 4.1 gives the keys to use when highlighting a filename.

Table 4.1
Keys for Highlighting Filenames

Key	Use
← →	Moves left or right one name in a line. Going past the end of a line moves to the end of the adjacent line.
↑ ↓	Moves up or down one line.
HOME END	Moves to the first or last filename.
F3 or Name	Switches between the single line and a full screen display of filenames.
↵ ENTER	Selects the highlighted filename.

> **TIP** The full screen display of the /File Retrieve command is a quick way to determine the names of worksheet files in the current directory. Simply execute the command and press the NAME (F3) key. Press CTRL-BREAK to return to Ready mode.

Using the single-line filename display, you view one line of filenames at a time. Pressing the F3 function key, called the NAME key, produces a full screen display of the filenames. Each line of the full screen display corresponds to a line visible in the single-line display. When you view files using the full screen display, the third line of the control panel contains the name of the highlighted file, the date and time it was last saved, and its size. After you have highlighted the desired file, press the ENTER key to retrieve it. ◄

After a worksheet has been retrieved, 1-2-3 remembers the name of the associated worksheet file. When you go to save the worksheet again using the /File Save command, 1-2-3 prompts you with this filename for the worksheet file. To update the file with the new worksheet contents, press the ENTER key and select the Replace option as described earlier.

TUTORIAL

In this tutorial, you learn the basics of how to manage files and worksheets. In particular, you practice choosing where to store your files; saving and retrieving files; and erasing a worksheet.

1 Set the directory. This book assumes that you will save your files on a floppy disk in drive A. If your current directory is not A:\, you first choose directory A:\ as the directory in which your files will be stored. In other situations, you can use these steps to choose some other directory in which to store your files.

Press	/	Activates the Main menu.
Press	F	Selects File.
Press	D	Selects Directory.

The "Enter current directory: A:\" message is on the second line of the control panel. The mode indicator displays *EDIT*. The current directory is assumed to be A:\; if not, you should change the directory to A:\ by typing A:\.

Press	↵ ENTER	Confirms A:\ is the current directory.

2 Save a new file. While you are entering information into a new worksheet, the worksheet is saved only temporarily in the computer memory. It is erased when the computer is turned off. Before turning the computer off, you should make a permanent copy of the worksheet by saving it as a worksheet file on a disk. You should have the worksheet you created in Topic 3 on the screen. If not, use Figure 3.3 as a guide to re-create it. Be sure the cell pointer is in cell A18. This worksheet file will be named REVENUE since, as you develop the worksheet, it will be doing a yearly revenue forecast for hardware products.

> **TIP** If no files are in the current directory, the response to the prompt is "A:\" and the mode indicator displays *EDIT.*

Press	/	Activates the Main menu.
Press	F	Selects File.
Press	S	Selects Save.

The "Enter name of file to save: A:*.wk1" message is on the second line of the control panel. The mode indicator displays *FILES*. A list of the files in the current directory is on the third line of the control panel. ◀

Type	REVENUE	Displays REVENUE on control panel.

The filename is REVENUE. Capital letters are optional.

Press	↵ ENTER

The mode indicator briefly displays *WAIT*. The worksheet is saved on the disk in drive A with the filename REVENUE. You return to cell A18 in the worksheet. As you will see, 1-2-3 has added the extension .WK1 to the filename you entered.

3 **Erase a worksheet.** To leave your current application and begin a new one, you erase the current worksheet. The /Worksheet Erase command replaces the current worksheet on the screen and in the computer memory with an empty worksheet. *Be sure to save the current worksheet first if you want to keep any changes you have made to it.* To start this section, the worksheet from the last section should still be on the screen.

Press	/	Activates the Main menu.
Press	W	Selects Worksheet.
Press	E	Selects Erase.

If you have forgotten to save the current worksheet, 1-2-3 allows you to change your mind about erasing it.

Press	Y	Selects Yes; confirms the decision to erase the worksheet.

The worksheet is erased. An empty worksheet with the cell pointer in cell A1 is on the screen.

4 **Retrieve a file.** To make changes to a file, you must first retrieve it. The retrieved worksheet replaces the current worksheet in the computer memory and on the screen. To start this section, an empty worksheet should be on your screen.

Press	/, F	Selects File.
Press	R	Selects Retrieve.

The "Name of file to retrieve: A:*.wk?" message is on the second line of the control panel. The names of the current files are listed in alphabetical order across the third line of the control panel. The names may extend beyond the edge of the screen, but the arrow keys bring them onto the screen. You can enter the name of the file to retrieve by typing it or highlighting it and then pressing the Enter key. The mode indicator displays *FILES*.

TIP To specify the file to retrieve using a mouse, move the mouse pointer to the desired filename and click the mouse button.

Type	REVENUE	Specifies REVENUE as the file to retrieve. ◀
Press	↵ ENTER	Retrieves REVENUE.

REVENUE is the current worksheet on the screen. It appears exactly the way it was when you saved it.

5 **Save changes.** When you make changes to a worksheet, they occur only in the worksheet and not in the file. To make the changes permanent, you must save the worksheet again. The REVENUE worksheet should be on the screen.

Move to	cell B3	
Type	250	
Press	↵ ENTER	Enters 250 into cell B3.
Press	/, F	Selects File.
Press	R, Y	Selects Retrieve, Yes.

The list of filenames is on the control panel. Now retrieve the REVENUE file.

Move to	REVENUE.WK1	
Press	↵ ENTER	REVENUE becomes the current worksheet.

The worksheet was not saved after the value was changed so that the value in cell B3 is still 225 not 250. The cell pointer is still in cell A18. You now change the value in cell B3 to 250 again and save the worksheet to make the change permanent.

Move to	cell B3
Type	250

Press	↵ENTER	Enters 250 into cell B3.
Press	/, F	Selects File.
Press	S	Selects Save.

Since this worksheet has already been named, the message on the second line of the control panel includes the name of the file: "Enter name of file to save: A:\REVENUE.WK1". The mode indicator displays *EDIT*.

Press	↵ENTER	Displays confirmation menu.
Press	R	Selects Replace.

You save the worksheet with the name unchanged. The new version of the worksheet file replaces the old version of the file on the disk. You now erase the worksheet and then retrieve the file to see that the change has been saved.

Press	/, W	Selects Worksheet.
Press	E	Selects Erase.
Press	Y	Selects Yes; erases the worksheet.
Press	/, F, R	Selects File, Retrieve.
Move to	REVENUE.WK1	Specifies REVENUE as the file to retrieve.
Press	↵ENTER	Retrieves the REVENUE worksheet.

Note that the value in cell B3 is now the 250. The cell pointer is in cell B3. The sum in cell B9, which you entered as a number, is incorrect. It did not adjust automatically when you changed the revenue value. So you must change it manually.

Move to	cell B9	
Type	1350	
Press	↵ENTER	Enters 1350 into cell B9.

You now save the worksheet with the correct values.

Press	/, F, S	Selects File, Save.
Press	↵ENTER	Confirms REVENUE as the filename.
Press	R	Selects Replace.

6 **Save the file using a different name.** Sometimes you need to save two (or more) different files from the same worksheet. One common reason is to create a template for future worksheets (Topic 7). Another reason is to have a version of the worksheet available for What-If analysis. You save the worksheet under a different name from the original file. The REVENUE worksheet is on the screen.

Press	/, F, S	Selects File, Save.
Type	QTRMAST	The filename is QTRMAST.
Press	↵ ENTER	Saves the worksheet using the filename QTRMAST.

The disk now contains two files created from the same worksheet—one with the name REVENUE and one with the name QTRMAST. Editing either one has no effect on the other. QTRMAST is used as a template for actual quarterly revenue in later sections.

Press	/, F, R	Selects File, Retrieve.

The list of files in the current directory is on the third line of the control panel. The filenames can also be displayed in a full screen display.

Press	F3	Activates the name feature.

The result is a full screen display of the names of all the worksheet files on the disk. You can retrieve a file from this display by highlighting the name of the file and pressing the Enter key. Note that both REVENUE.WK1 and QTRMAST.WK1 are there.

Press	CTRL-BREAK	Leaves the menus; returns to Ready mode.

PROCEDURE SUMMARY

SPECIFYING WHERE TO STORE FILES

To specify the current directory:

Activate the Main menu.	/
Select File.	F
Select Directory.	D
Type the directory pathname.	(your input—in this book, A:\)
Enter the input.	↵ ENTER

SAVING A WORKSHEET TO A FILE

To save a worksheet with an unused filename:

Activate the Main menu.	/
Select File.	F
Select Save.	S
Type the filename.	(your input)
Enter the input.	↵ ENTER

To save a worksheet with a filename in use:

Activate the Main menu.	/
Select File.	F
Select Save.	S
Select the filename by one of the following means:	
Confirm the current filename.	↵ ENTER
Type or highlight the name of another file.	(your input)
Enter the input.	↵ ENTER
Select Replace.	R

ERASING A WORKSHEET FROM MAIN MEMORY

Activate the Main menu.	/
Select Worksheet.	W
Select Erase.	E
Select Yes.	Y

RETRIEVING A WORKSHEET

Activate the Main menu.	/
Select File.	F
Select Retrieve.	R
Type or highlight the filename.	(your input)
Enter the input.	↵ ENTER

EXERCISES

4A Create a small worksheet, save the worksheet to a file, and retrieve the worksheet from the file.

In most of the remaining exercises, you are asked to save the worksheet on a file using a specific filename. The coding for the filenames is ExxY, where E is exercise, xx is the number of the topic, and Y is the part number for which the file must be saved. By saving worksheets using this naming convention, you can return to a specific exercise and see the results.

1. Enter your name in cell B1.
2. Enter the current date in cell B2.
3. Enter the text "Stock No." in cell A5.
4. Center the text "Item" in cell B5.
5. Enter the text "Inventory" in cell C5
6. Enter the text "AX123" in cell A6.
7. Enter the text "Coats" in cell B6.
8. Enter the number 367 in cell C6.
9. Enter the text "BA410" in cell A7.
10. Enter the text "Dresses" in cell B7.
11. Enter the number 395 in cell C7.
12. Save the worksheet to your data disk using the filename E04A.
13. Erase the worksheet from your screen.
14. Retrieve the E04A file.
15. Enter the number 479 in cell C7.
16. Save the worksheet to your data disk using the filename E04A.
17. Erase the worksheet from your screen.
18. Retrieve the E04A file.

4B Create a small worksheet, save the worksheet to a file, and retrieve the worksheet from the file.

1. Complete the instructions in Exercise 3B again.
2. Save the worksheet using the filename E04B.
3. Erase the worksheet from your screen.
4. Retrieve the E04B file.

Printing a Worksheet

> **TIP** Sending a report to a file creates a file with the extension .PRN. This file can be read into your word processor and edited to create an enhanced report. Also, release 2.3 of 1-2-3 has an add-in program, WYSIWYG, for enhancing reports.

> **TIP** The /Worksheet Global Default Printer command is used to set the defaults for the options displayed in the Print Settings sheet.

CONCEPTS

Although 1-2-3 displays your worksheets on the screen, most worksheet results are distributed as printed reports using the /Print command. This topic discusses the basics of the /Print command, leaving the more advanced details for later (Topic 14). Also included is a presentation of ranges, a fundamental 1-2-3 concept.

Initiating the Print Process

55

After you select the /Print command from the Main menu, 1-2-3 displays a menu providing two options, Printer and File, for the destination of the output report. The Printer option specifies that the output should be sent to the printer. The File option directs the output to a **print file**. Note that selecting either destination only indicates where the report will go; it does not actually print the report. ◀

Once you have selected the report destination, the worksheet area is replaced by a sheet of **Print Settings** that give the current settings of various print options. The Destination option reflects your choice, Printer or File, from the first menu. Initially some options such as Margins and Page Length have been filled in using default values. Most options are blank. Pressing the F6 function key, called the WINDOW key, switches the screen between the Print Settings display and the worksheet area. ◀

Simultaneously 1-2-3 displays a menu in the control panel. You use the commands within this menu, called the **print commands**, to change the print settings and then print your reports. Table 5.1 summarizes these commands.

Table 5.1
The Print Commands

Command	Use
Range	Specifies the range of cells to be printed.
Line	Inserts a blank line in the output report.
Page	Moves the printer to the top of a new page.
Options	Accesses a submenu of additional options.
Align	Resets 1-2-3's internal line and page counters.
Go	Prints the current print range.
Quit	Ends the /Print command and returns to Ready mode.

Specifying the Print Range

56

Before printing from your worksheet, you must specify the **print range**, a rectangular block of cells containing the data for your report.

The concept of a **range** appears frequently in 1-2-3. The term designates any rectangular block of adjacent cells. Ranges can consist of cells within a single column or row or even a single cell. For printing purposes, however, ranges usually consist of blocks of cells from multiple rows and columns. Although this topic focuses on the use of ranges in the /Print command, the techniques it introduces apply equally well to many other 1-2-3 activities.

Ranges, including the Print Range, can be specified in one of two ways: by using the cell pointer to highlight the cells in the range or by typing the **range address**. A range address consists of the cell addresses of two diagonally opposite corners of the range separated by two periods. Normally the upper left and lower right corners are chosen. The address B2..B10 indicates a column of cells extending from row 2 to row 10 in worksheet column B. If we think of the two periods as standing for the word "to," we would speak of the range of cells "B2 to B10." The range address A1..H20 ("A1 to H20") denotes the rectangle of cells that is visible when you first start 1-2-3. The address B1..B1 denotes the range consisting of the single cell B1. ◀

> **TIP** Being able to distinguish between a cell address, B1, and a range address, B1..B1, is very important. As discussed later, they behave quite differently when used with 1-2-3 commands.

Instead of typing the range address, you can use an alternative method called **pointing**. In this method you use the movement keys to expand the cell pointer so that it points to, or highlights, the rectangle of cells you want for the range. Pointing is generally the preferred method for selecting ranges, and it is the one emphasized in this book.

Selecting ranges by pointing is a fundamental skill in using 1-2-3. The basic steps for pointing to the initial print range are described here. Depending on 1-2-3's initial suggestion when you start a command or function, different combinations of these steps are used to select ranges in other contexts. Pointing to ranges is illustrated thoroughly in the tutorials.

To point to the initial print range:

1. You select the Range option from the Print menu.

   1-2-3 provides the *cell* address of the current cell as the suggested response. The mode indicator displays *POINT*. The Print Settings sheet disappears and the worksheet area appears.

2. You use the movement keys to move the cell pointer to the upper left corner of the print range.

   In the control panel, the displayed cell address corresponds to the location of the cell pointer. ◀

> **TIP** Before you execute a command that will require a range, it is generally useful to position the cell pointer in the upper left corner of the range you will be specifying.

3. You press the period key to **anchor** the cell pointer.

   In the control panel, this changes the cell address to a *range* address. For example, if the cell pointer was in cell A1, the address in the control panel changes from the cell address A1 to the range address A1..A1. Once the cell pointer is anchored, that is, when a range address appears

TIP To highlight the print range using a mouse, move the mouse pointer to the upper left corner of the print, hold down the mouse button, and move the mouse pointer to the lower right corner of the print range. Then click the mouse button.

in the control panel, using the movement keys expands the cell pointer to highlight a range.

4. You use the movement keys to highlight, that is, "point to," the desired print range.

   The cell you were in when you anchored the cell pointer forms one corner of the range and remains fixed in place. This is called the **anchored cell**. The corner opposite it is termed the **free cell** because it is free to move in response to the movement keys. The highlight covers the rectangular range that has the anchored cell and the free cell at opposite corners. In the control panel, 1-2-3 displays the range address of this range. Moving the free cell to the lower right corner of the desired range expands the highlight to cover the entire range.

5. You press the ENTER key to assign the highlighted range to the print range.

   The Print Settings sheet is redisplayed with the print range filled in.

Once you specify a print range for a worksheet, 1-2-3 remembers it for the current session. If you save the worksheet after you have specified the range, 1-2-3 remembers it in later sessions. If this previous print range is correct, you do not need to specify it again. If you do select the Range option from the Print menu, 1-2-3 highlights the previous range definition. Press the ENTER key to leave the range unchanged.

On the other hand, you may want a completely different print range or you may need to make changes in the current print range. If the anchored cell is at the corner of the new range, you can point to the new range by moving the free cell. If the anchored cell is no longer at the corner of the range, you can press the ESCAPE key to convert the range address in the control panel to the cell address of the anchored cell. For example, pressing the ESCAPE key changes the range address A1..B9 to the cell address A1. Simultaneously the expanded cell pointer on the screen is replaced by the normal cell pointer located in what was the anchored cell. You then proceed from step 2 to point to the new range.

TIP If the worksheet contains long labels that are only partially displayed in the print range, 1-2-3 prints only those portions of the labels that appear in the cells in the print range.

TIP The horizontal location of the printed material on the page and the number of lines on the page are controlled by the margins. You can also define headers and footers that appear on the top and bottom of each page (Topic 14).

Printing the Worksheet

57

Once you have specified the print range, you tell 1-2-3 to begin printing the report by selecting the Go command. The mode indicator displays the blinking message *WAIT*, and the report starts to print.

Assuming you are at the beginning of the page, 1-2-3 skips several lines and begins to print the information that is visible in the print range. Each row in the print range produces one line in the output report.

If the print range contains more rows than can fit on one page, 1-2-3 prints as many rows as it can, leaves several blank lines, and begins a new page. This continues until all rows in the print range have been printed. If the print range is too wide for one page, 1-2-3 prints only the information that fits within the margins, but it retains the remaining information to be printed later. Then, after 1-2-3 has printed the initial portions of all rows in the print range, it moves to the top of a new page and begins printing the remaining portions. You can place the two sets of pages side by side to view the entire report.

> **TIP** Since many printers have internal storage that allows them to receive more text from the computer than they have thus far printed, 1-2-3 may return to the Print Command menu while the printer is still printing. You can continue working in 1-2-3 while the printer prints.

Controlling the Printer

(57)

After the printing is finished, 1-2-3 displays the Print Command menu. At this point it is ready to accept additional commands. ◀

You usually select the Page command followed by the Quit command. The Page command finishes the report, bringing the printer to the top of a new page or ejecting the last page of the report. The Quit command returns you to Ready mode. Sometimes you may want to print more than one range in the same report or the same range several times. After the first range finishes printing, you specify the second print range as described earlier. You can then either immediately print the second range by selecting Go or you can first adjust the printer by using the Page or Line commands. Choosing the Page command moves the printer to a new page before printing the range, whereas each use of the Line command inserts one blank row in the output report. This process is then repeated for all the ranges to be printed.

One other aspect of printing sometimes causes problems for the beginning 1-2-3 user. As it is printing, 1-2-3 keeps track of how many lines it has printed so that it knows when to move to the top of a new page. It remembers this number even after you leave the Print menu. If you use the /Print commands as described here, the printer will always be at the beginning of a new page after each report and 1-2-3 will know it is there. However, if you forget to issue the Page command, the paper jams, or you manually adjust the position of the paper in the printer for any reason, 1-2-3 may not know the true position of the printer on the page. Subsequent reports may then print with page breaks in the middle of the page. You use the Align command to tell 1-2-3 whenever you have manually adjusted the paper to the top of the page in your printer. Prior to printing any report, you should ensure that the printer is at the top of the page and execute the Align command as soon as you enter the Print Command menu.

TUTORIAL

In this tutorial, you learn how to print a section of the worksheet. The crucial step is choosing the print range, that is, the block of cells to be printed, or the body of the report. Choosing ranges is an essential skill since it is an important step in using many of the 1-2-3 commands. If the REVENUE worksheet is not on the screen, retrieve the REVENUE file before you begin this tutorial. The cell pointer should still be in cell B9. Be sure the printer is turned on and on line.

1 **Initiate the print process.** First select where to send the output—directly to the printer or to a file to be printed later.

Press	/	Activates the Main menu.
Press	P	Selects Print.
Press	P	Selects Printer.

You get a display of current print settings. Adjust the paper so that the printer is at the top of a page. Make sure 1-2-3 is at the top of a page by resetting the line counter.

Press	A	Selects Align; sets line and page counters to 0.

2 **Specify a print range.** You first print the main body of the worksheet. You choose A1..B9 for the print range. It is selected by pointing, although it could also be done by typing. Figure 5.1 displays the steps in the pointing process.

Figure 5.1
Pointing to a Range

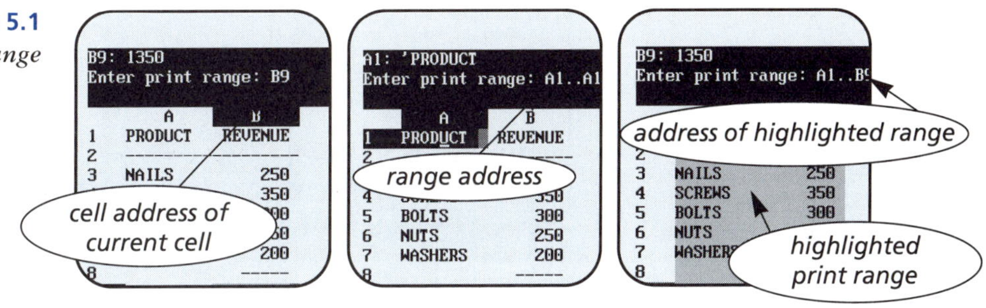

Press	R	Selects Range; mode indicator displays *POINT*.

The message "Enter print range: B9" appears on the control panel. B9 is the current cell.

Press	HOME	Moves cell pointer to cell A1.

The cell address in the control panel is now A1.

Press	.	Anchors range with a period.

The message is now "Enter print range: A1..A1." The cell address A1 has been converted to a range address A1..A1. Note that 1-2-3 uses two periods in a range address although you typed in only one.

Press	END, →, END, ↓	Expands cell pointer to Total Revenue cell, B9.

The range with A1 and B9 as its corners is highlighted on the screen. The range address, A1..B9, is in the control panel.

Press	↵ENTER	Locks in range selection; displays Print Settings.

3 **Print.** Once you have specified the print range, select Go to print it. Before printing, you should check the Print Settings display to verify that all the options are chosen correctly (Figure 5.2).

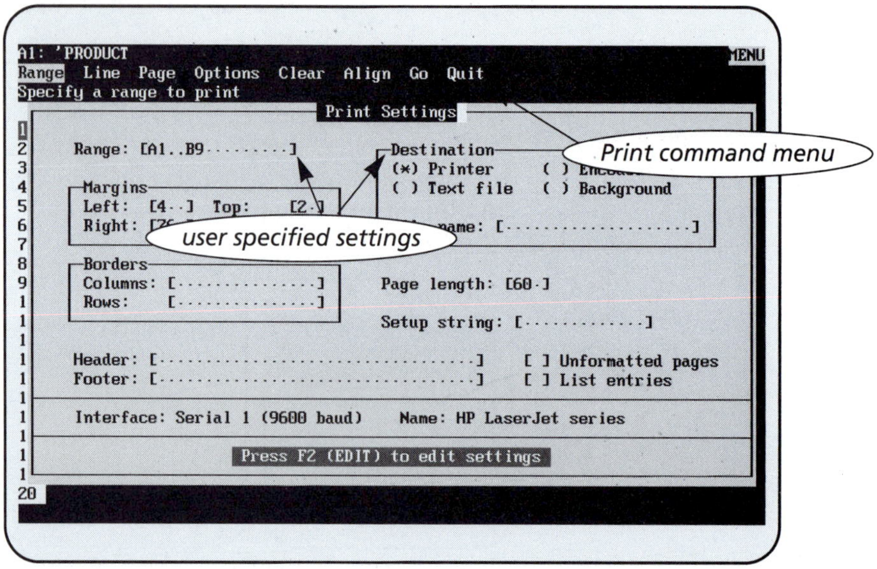

Figure 5.2
Print Settings

Press	G	Selects Go; prints range.
Press	P	Selects Page.

The printer advances to the top of the next page of paper so that the next printout will begin on the top of a page. ◄

Press	Q	Selects Quit; leaves Print menu.

4 **Change the print range.** In this section, you select several different print ranges and print them out.

Press	/, P, P, A	Selects Print, Printer, Align.

The Print Settings screen has A1..B9 as the print range. 1-2-3 remembers the print range you selected.

Press	R	Selects Range.

The message is "Enter print range: A1..B9." The cells from A1 to B9 are highlighted on the screen. You now select a new range, which includes the footnotes. You do this by typing for the only time in the tutorials. ◄

TIP If you end your report with a page break (Topic 14), you should omit this step in the print process. If the paper is not in continuous feed mode, the Page command ejects the last page of the report.

TIP Ranges can always be chosen by typing. However, pointing is a much better way to choose ranges because it minimizes mistakes.

> **TIP** 1-2-3 determines what to print by the data that is highlighted on the screen rather than by what is in the underlying cells. This is another advantage to pointing. You can decide when the range is correct by what you see highlighted on the screen rather than by the range address in the prompt response.

Type	A1..B18	Specifies new range.
Press	↵ENTER	Locks in selection; displays Print Settings.
Press	G, P	Selects Go, Page.

You print the new range and go to the top of the next page. Note that not all of the "Prepared by Roger Jones" label is printed. You reenter the print range by pointing to include all of the label. ◀

Press	R	Selects Range.

The previously selected range, A1..B18, is highlighted on the screen and the address is on the control panel. You now expand the highlight to include the entire footnote.

Press	→	Moves free cell to cell C18.

The highlighted range is now A1..C18, which covers all the information on the screen.

Press	↵ENTER	Locks in selection.
Press	G, P, Q	Selects Go, Page, Quit.

When you save the worksheet, 1-2-3 saves the last print range as part of the file.

Press	/, F, S, ↵ENTER, R	Selects File, Save, REVENUE.WK1, Replace.

The worksheet, including the last specified print range, is saved using the filename REVENUE. This modified worksheet replaces the old file REVENUE. This completes the initial tutorial on printing. Topic 14 covers advanced printing techniques.

PROCEDURE SUMMARY

INITIATING THE PRINT PROCESS

To print to a printer:

Activate the Main menu.	/
Select Print.	P
Select Printer.	P

SPECIFYING THE PRINT RANGE

These techniques for selecting a print range are used in other contexts that require you to select a range.

To select the first range to be printed:

Access the Print menu.	/, P, P
Select Range.	R
Move the cell pointer to the upper left corner of the range.	(pointer-movement keys)
Anchor the cell pointer.	.
Highlight the range by expanding the cell pointer to the lower right corner of the range.	(pointer-movement keys)
Lock in the selection.	↵ ENTER

To change the print range to one using the same anchored cell:

Access the Print menu.	/, P, P
Select Range.	R
Highlight the range by expanding the cell pointer to the lower right corner of the range.	(pointer-movement keys)
Lock in the selection.	↵ ENTER

To change the print range to one using a new anchored cell:

Access the Print menu.	/, P, P
Select Range.	R
Convert the range address to a cell address.	ESC
Move the cell pointer to the upper left corner of the new range.	(pointer-movement keys)
Anchor the cell pointer.	.
Highlight the range by expanding the cell pointer to the lower right corner of the range.	(pointer-movement keys)
Lock in the selection.	↵ ENTER

To specify the print range to be printed using a mouse:

Access the Print menu.	/, P, P
Select Range.	R
Move the mouse pointer to the upper left corner of the range.	(mouse)
Hold down the mouse button.	(mouse)
Move the mouse pointer to the lower right corner of the range.	(mouse)
Lock in the selection.	click mouse button or ↵ ENTER

PRINTING THE WORKSHEET

Be sure the printer is on and at the top of a page.	
Access the Print menu.	/, P, P
Select Align.	A
Select Range.	R
Specify the print range.	(your input)
Lock in the selection.	↵ ENTER
Select Go.	G
Select Page if the report does not end with a page break.	P
Select Quit.	Q

CONTROLLING THE PRINTER

Access the Print menu.	/, P, P
Take one or more of the following steps.	
Set the 1-2-3 line and page counter to 0.	
Select Align.	A
Advance the paper to the top of the next page.	
Select Page.	P
Advance the paper one line.	
Select Line.	L

EXERCISES

5A Retrieve a worksheet from a file and then print it.

1. Retrieve the worksheet stored in the E04A file.
2. Print the worksheet.
3. Skip to the top of the next page.
4. Print the range of cells that includes your name and the date.

5B Retrieve a worksheet from a file and then print it.

1. Retrieve the E04B file.
2. Print the worksheet.

Entering Formulas

CONCEPTS Although electronic worksheets are excellent tools for entering and printing information arranged in rows and columns, their true utility lies in their ability to store formulas that perform calculations on the data in the cells. Prior to the introduction of these programs, countless individuals spent large portions of their time performing analyses with pencil and paper or with calculators. Then, if any component of the analysis changed, many of the calculations would need to be redone. To minimize errors, these calculations needed to be checked and rechecked with each change.

Now spreadsheet programs allow you to store the formulas for the calculations in worksheet cells. If any values or assumptions change, you need only enter the new numbers or formulas and 1-2-3 automatically recalculates the new results for the entire worksheet. The need to control errors still exists. However, it focuses on the validation of the worksheet formulas and data, rather than on computational accuracy.

Calculating in 1-2-3

TIP In release 2.3 of 1-2-3, you can also create **linking formulas** that draw on information contained in other worksheets.

1-2-3 performs calculations by using **formulas** that you enter into cells. Formulas are expressions that specify the calculations to be performed and the data to be used in the calculations. 1-2-3 formulas look very similar to the formulas used in mathematics, business, and science. In this topic, we focus on arithmetic formulas. Additional methods of calculation are discussed in Topics 12 and 15. Table 6.1 shows the symbols that 1-2-3 uses to represent the basic arithmetic operations and the order in which calculations are performed in formulas containing more than one operation. ◀

Table 6.1
1-2-3 Symbols for Arithmetic Operations

Symbol	Operation	Order
^	Exponentiation (raising to a power)	1
–	Negation	2
*	Multiplication	3
/	Division	3
+	Addition	4
–	Subtraction	4

1-2-3 formulas can perform calculations with information included in the formula itself or with values contained in other cells in the worksheet. For example, the formula 0.07*20 in cell B5 (Figure 6.1a) calculates a 7 percent sales tax on a $20 purchase. Here the numbers used in the calculation are entered directly into the formula. Note that a cell containing a formula displays the calculated result, rather than the formula, in the worksheet area. If the cell containing the formula is the current cell, the formula is visible in the current cell contents in the control panel.

In practice, formulas are useful because they can perform calculations with the data contained in other worksheet cells. If the purchase amount is stored in cell B1, you would use the formula 0.07*B1 in cell B5 (Figure 6.1b) to multiply the 7 percent rate times the value in cell B1. This formula contains a **constant** value, the number 0.07, and a **cell reference**, B1. 1-2-3 uses the value in cell B1 when it performs the calculation. Finally, if cell B3 contains the tax rate, you could enter the formula +B3*B1 into cell B5 (Figure 6.1c) to perform the same calculation. The formula multiplies the rate in cell B3 times the purchase amount in cell B1 and displays the result in cell B5. ◀

TIP The initial + in +B1*B3 indicates that this is a formula. 1-2-3 would interpret an entry such as B1*B3 as a label because it starts with a letter.

Figure 6.1
Alternate Formulas for Sales Tax

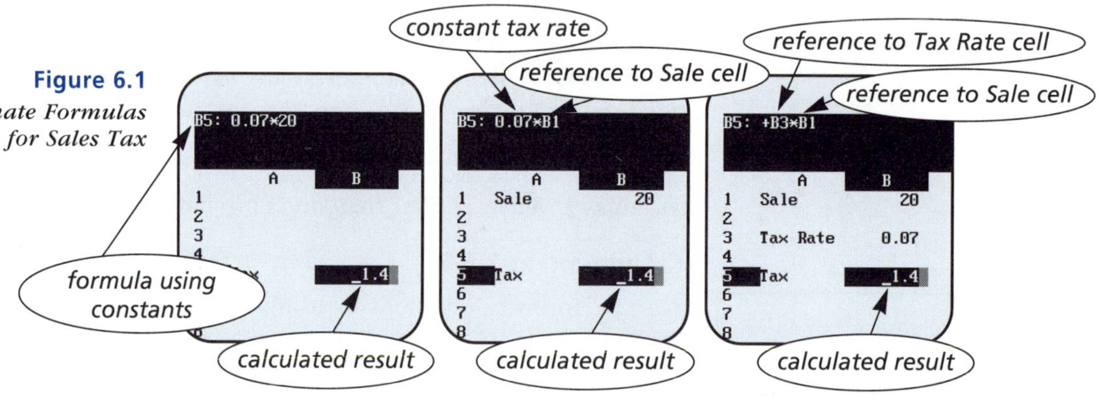

When a formula contains more than one operation, the order in which the operations are performed may be important. 1-2-3 follows the commonly accepted conventions given in Table 6.1. Exponentiations are performed first, then negations, then multiplications and divisions, and finally additions and subtractions. If a series of similar operations such as a series of multiplications and divisions must be performed, it is performed from left to right.

You can override this standard sequence of calculation by enclosing expressions within parentheses. 1-2-3 calculates expressions within parentheses first. You can have as many levels of parentheses as you need. It is good practice to use parentheses freely in your formulas to clarify the order in which the calculations are to be performed even if the parentheses are not strictly required. ◀

TIP Fractions can be included in formulas as decimal values or as calculations. For example, the decimal value 1.25 could also be entered as (1+(1/4)), where the parentheses are used to emphasize the sequence of the calculation.

Entering Formulas

To enter a formula, you first move the cell pointer to the cell that is to contain the formula. Then you enter the formula either by **typing** or **pointing**. Although both of these methods require you to type numbers and other symbols into formulas, they differ in the way cell references are entered. In the typing method, you type the cell references. In the pointing method, you highlight cells with the cell pointer and 1-2-3 enters the cell reference into the formula for you.

In both methods, you begin the formula by typing. 1-2-3 recognizes any expression that begins with a number or any of the numeric symbols + - @ (. # or $ as being a formula. 1-2-3 interprets an expression that begins with a cell address such as B1*B3 as a label. To enter this formula, you may either surround it in parentheses and enter (B1*B3) or precede it by a plus sign as +B1*B3. This book uses the plus sign method.

When you are finished building your formula and try to store it into the cell, 1-2-3 examines the formula for errors. Typical errors include spaces in the middle or at the end and unmatched parentheses. If your entry contains an error that makes the formula invalid, 1-2-3 beeps and puts you in Edit mode. This allows you to correct the formula (Topic 7). Alternatively you can press the ESCAPE key twice to get back to Ready mode. (The first ESCAPE erases the text but leaves you in Edit mode. The second ESCAPE gets you back to Ready mode.)

Note, however, that if you mistype your entry but it is still a valid formula, 1-2-3 stores it even though it is not what you intended. Thus, if you want to add cells B1 and B3 together but instead type +B1+B2, 1-2-3 accepts the entry, but your worksheet will be incorrect.

Recalculating Worksheets

When the value of any cell in the worksheet changes, 1-2-3 automatically recalculates the formulas in all cells that are affected by the change and displays the new results. As part of this process, 1-2-3 also determines the correct order in which to calculate the cells.

Thus, if the formula +B3*B1 is in cell B5 and you enter a new rate in cell B3, 1-2-3 automatically recomputes the sales tax in cell B5. If, in addition, cell B7 contains the formula +B1+B5, which adds the purchase price and the sales tax, 1-2-3 calculates a new total in cell B7 even though cell B7 does not directly reference cell B3. 1-2-3 knows to perform this calculation after it computes the tax in cell B5. The enormous speed of personal computers makes the recalculation of the formulas almost instantaneous for small worksheets, and you are hardly aware that the recalculation is taking place.

It is this ability to automatically recalculate the formulas you store in your worksheets that provides many of the advantages of spreadsheet programs. To take advantage of this ability, you should design your worksheets with cells to contain the input values. The formulas that use these values should be placed in separate cells and should access the input values via cell references within the formulas as was done in Figure 6.1c. In this way you can easily change the input data without having to modify the formulas themselves. In addition, by placing input values in cells rather than in formulas, you can easily view these values on the screen and include them in your reports. For example, in Figure 6.1c, having the sales in cell B1 and the tax rate in cell B3 rather than entered directly into the formula helps the worksheet user see what values are being used. It also makes the worksheet flexible in that you can change the sales and rate easily.

Building Formulas by Pointing

69

Realistic worksheets may contain hundreds of formulas. For the worksheet to be correct, all of these formulas must be correct. The process of building a worksheet, therefore, requires a very high degree of accuracy. To achieve these levels of accuracy, experienced 1-2-3 users rely on pointing techniques and the /Copy command (Topic 9) for building formulas. With the pointing method, you include cell references in your formulas by pointing to them with the cell pointer rather than by typing their addresses.

You start entering a formula by typing some character that 1-2-3 interprets as beginning a value. When you reach the point in the formula that requires a cell reference, you use any movement key to move the cell pointer toward the desired cell. 1-2-3 includes the address of the cell pointer at the end of the entry in the control panel. Simultaneously the mode indicator switches from *VALUE* to *POINT*. As you continue to move the cell pointer, the cell address in the formula changes to agree with the cell pointer position. Thus, when the cell pointer is "pointing" to the cell you want, 1-2-3 has already included its address in the formula. If the formula is then complete, you press the ENTER key to store it in the cell. If not, you type the next symbol. The cell pointer returns to the current cell, and the mode indicator returns to *VALUE*.

> **TIP** 1-2-3 always returns you to the current cell when you type in a new symbol after pointing. Thus building large worksheets can require a lot of movement. The use of windows (Topic 13) can simplify this dramatically.

To enter the formula +B3*B1 into cell B5, you place the cell pointer in cell B5 and type the plus sign (Figure 6.2a). Then you press the UP ARROW key, moving the cell pointer toward cell B3. 1-2-3 includes the cell pointer address, B4, after the plus sign (Figure 6.2b). 1-2-3 adjusts the cell address as you move to B3 (Figure 6.2c). When you reach cell B3, you type the multiplication sign, *, which locks the cell address B3 into the formula and returns the cell pointer to cell B5 (Figure 6.2d). You then move the cell pointer to cell B1 to complete the formula (Figure 6.2e) and press the ENTER key (Figure 6.2f) to store it. ◀

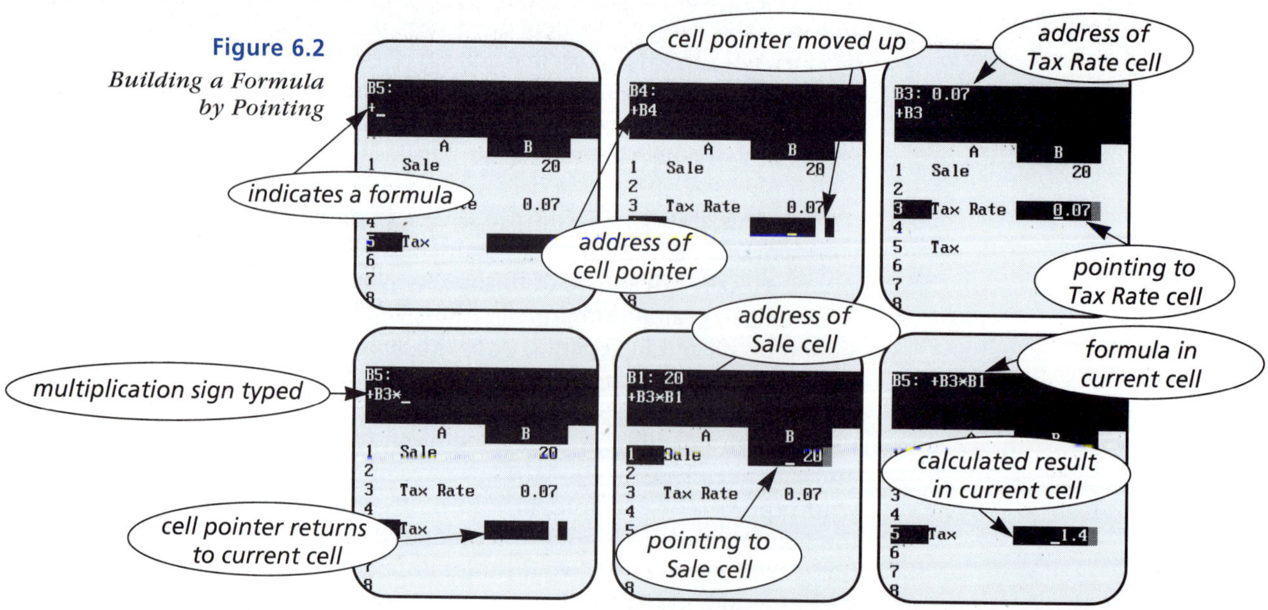

Figure 6.2
Building a Formula by Pointing

> **TIP** Pointing techniques become more important as worksheets get large. Large worksheets are the norm in actual practice even though this book mainly uses small worksheets to illustrate various points.

What do you gain by pointing? Obviously, because 1-2-3 types in cell addresses for you, you eliminate that task and the chance of making a typographical error. More subtly however, pointing also frees you from determining cell locations. When you select a cell to be included in a formula, you recognize it by its role in the worksheet. For example, you select a cell because it contains the sales figure or the tax rate. When you place the cell pointer in the desired cell, 1-2-3 determines the cell address and inserts it in the formula for you. In contrast, when you type a formula, you must look at the border of the worksheet to determine the address of the cell. You must also remember this address when you return to enter it into the formula if the selected cell and the cell containing the formula are not both visible on the screen. This process is time consuming and error prone. ◀

TUTORIAL

In this tutorial, you enter some simple formulas primarily by pointing. As you start the tutorial, the REVENUE worksheet should be on the screen.

Note: From now on in the tutorials, we generally use the phrase "Moves to xx" instead of "Moves cell pointer to cell xx," where xx is the cell address. We will also save the standard REVENUE worksheet under the name REVxx, where xx is the topic number. If you wish to redo a tutorial, you can restore the worksheet as it was at the end of the previous tutorial.

> **TIP** In the worksheet area, you cannot distinguish between values that have been entered as numbers and values that are the results of computations. One way to tell which value is in the cell is to look at the current cell contents.

1 **Calculate in 1-2-3.** You can use 1-2-3 as a calculator. Type the formula you want evaluated into a cell. The result appears on the screen. Here you use the computer to add the product revenue values.

Move to	B9	
Type	250+350+300+250+200	Mode indicator displays *VALUE*.
Press	↵ ENTER	B9 displays 1350.

1-2-3 sums the numbers and displays the result on the screen. The formula appears in the control panel. ◀

2 **Build a formula using cell addresses.** The sum in B9 does not change if you change any of the product revenues. To have the computer automatically recalculate the sum when changes are made to the values, the formula must use the cell addresses rather than the numbers. This first time you build the formula by typing.

Type	B3+B4+B5+B6+B7	
Press	↵ ENTER	B3+B4+B5+B6+B7 appears in B9.

> **TIP** Recall that the first keystroke in an entry determines whether it is a label or a value. You must use a special character to begin a formula that would otherwise begin with a cell address. In the tutorials you usually use a plus sign (+).

> **TIP** To select a cell to include in a formula using a mouse, move the mouse pointer to the cell and click the mouse button.

Since you started the input with a letter "B," the entry is a label not a formula. Therefore the entry is displayed on the screen as it was typed. ◀

Type	+	Mode indicator displays *VALUE*.
Type	B3+B4+B5+B6+B7	
Press	↵ ENTER	B9 displays 1350.

The result of the calculation is displayed on the screen; the formula is shown in the current cell contents. As with ranges, it is usually better to enter formulas by pointing. You now reenter the formula by pointing. This first time we give you the steps in detail.

Type	+	Mode indicator displays *VALUE*.

Watch the screen while you press the Up Arrow. The cell pointer moves up, and 1-2-3 changes the formula on the control panel accordingly.

Press	↑ six times	Moves cell pointer to B3; mode indicator displays *POINT*. ◀

Pointer is in B3. Formula on second line of control panel is +B3.

Type	+	Moves cell pointer to B9; mode indicator displays *VALUE*.

Second line of control panel displays the partially built formula +B3+.

Press	↑ five times	Moves cell pointer to B4; formula is +B3+B4.
Type	+	Moves cell pointer to B9; formula is +B3+B4+.
Press	↑ four times	Moves cell pointer to B5; formula is +B3+B4+B5.
Type	+	Moves cell pointer to B9; formula is +B3+B4+B5+.
Press	↑ three times	Moves cell pointer to B6; formula is +B3+B4+B5+B6.
Type	+	Moves cell pointer to B9; formula is +B3+B4+B5+B6+.
Press	↑ twice	Moves cell pointer to B7.

> **TIP** To enter a formula using a mouse, input the formula. Then move the mouse pointer to the control panel and click the mouse button.

The formula is now complete. The cell pointer is in cell B7. The second line of the control panel displays +B3+B4+B5+B6+B7. You enter the formula into cell B9.

Press	↵ ENTER	B9 displays 1350, the calculated result. ◀

The formula is stored in the cell. The result of the calculation is displayed in the worksheet area.

3 **Recalculate results.** In this section, you see the effect of changing the product revenue values on the sum in cell B9.

Move to	B3	
Type	275	
Press	↵ ENTER	B9 displays 1375.

When the values in cells that the formula uses are changed, 1-2-3 recalculates the formula and displays the new result in the worksheet.

Press	↓	Moves to B4.
Type	375	
Press	↵ ENTER	B9 displays 1400.

4 **Use other arithmetic operations.** You now build formulas using some other arithmetic operations. Your goal here is the worksheet in Figure 6.3. You fill some of the cells you left blank earlier with these new formulas and with the labels for the new data. You first enter the labels.

Move to	A9	

You change TOTAL to GROSS for gross revenue.

Type	GROSS	
Press	↓	Enters "GROSS" in A9; moves to A10.

You enter a label for revenue adjustments. The label is indented two spaces by pressing the Spacebar twice.

Press	SPACEBAR twice	
Type	ADJUST	
Press	↓ twice	Enters " ADJUST." in A10; moves to A12.

TIP

Revenue adjustments arise from bad debts, product returns, and so on. They are computed as a percentage of gross revenue. We assume the value 20% and enter it in a separate cell. This way the assumption is displayed and easily changed.

You now enter labels for net revenue, gross adjustments (indented two spaces), and revenue adjustments. ◀

Type	NET	
Press	↓	Enters "NET"; moves to A13.
Type	SPACEBAR twice, % GROSS	
Press	↓ twice	Enters " % GROSS" in A13; moves to A15.
Type	REV ADJ %	
Press	→	Enters "REV ADJ %" in A15; moves to B15.
Type	20	
Press	↑ five times	Enters 20; moves to B10.

You now enter the formula to calculate revenue adjustments using pointing. When entering cells in formulas by pointing, you use the role the cell plays in the worksheet more than its address in selecting it.

Type	+	Begins formula.
Press	↑	Enters gross revenue, B9, in formula.

The formula is +B9. The cell pointer is in B9.

TIP

At times, particularly as you first practice the pointing technique, you may create some strange expressions as you try to build a formula. Remember that you can always cancel your input and return to Ready mode to start over by pressing ESC a sufficient number of times.

Type	*(	Enters multiplication sign; returns to B10.
Press	END, ↓	Enters revenue adjustment percent, B15, in formula.
Type	/100)	Converts percent to decimal; returns to B10.

The formula is +B9*(B15/100).

Press	↵ ENTER	Enters formula in B10; B10 displays 280. ◀

You enter a partial underlining, right aligned, to separate revenue adjustments from net revenue.

Press	↓	Moves to B11.
Type	"_____	
Press	↓	Enters "_____; moves to B12.

Net revenue is gross revenue minus revenue adjustments.

Type	+	Begins formula.
Press	↑ three times	Moves to gross revenue, B9.
Type	–	Enters subtraction sign; returns to B12.
Press	↑ twice	Moves to adjustments, B10.

The formula is +B9–B10.

Press	↵ ENTER	Enters formula in B12.

B12 displays 1120. Percent of gross revenue is computed by multiplying 100 times net revenue divided by gross revenue.

Press	↓	Moves to B13.
Type	+100*	Begins formula.

A plus sign is not required since 100 is a number.

Press	↑	Moves to net revenue, B12.
Type	/	Enters division sign.
Press	↑ four times	Moves to gross revenue, B9.
Press	↵ ENTER	Enters formula in B13.

B13 displays 80. You will now change some of the revenue values. Note the corresponding changes in the values computed by the formulas in cells B9, B10, B12, and B13.

TIP Even though cells B10, B12, and B13 do not contain B3 in their formulas, their values change when the value in B3 is changed. When the value in a cell is changed, all formulas that depend on that cell, even indirectly, are recalculated, and the new values are displayed.

Move to	B3	
Type	225	
Press	↓	Enters 225; moves to B4.
Type	350	
Press	↵ ENTER	Enters 350.

The gross revenue, 1325, is displayed in B9. Adjustments, 265, are displayed in B10. Net revenue, 1060, is displayed in B12. Percent of gross revenue, 80, is displayed in B13. Your worksheet should look like Figure 6.3. ◄

Figure 6.3
Revenue: Formulas

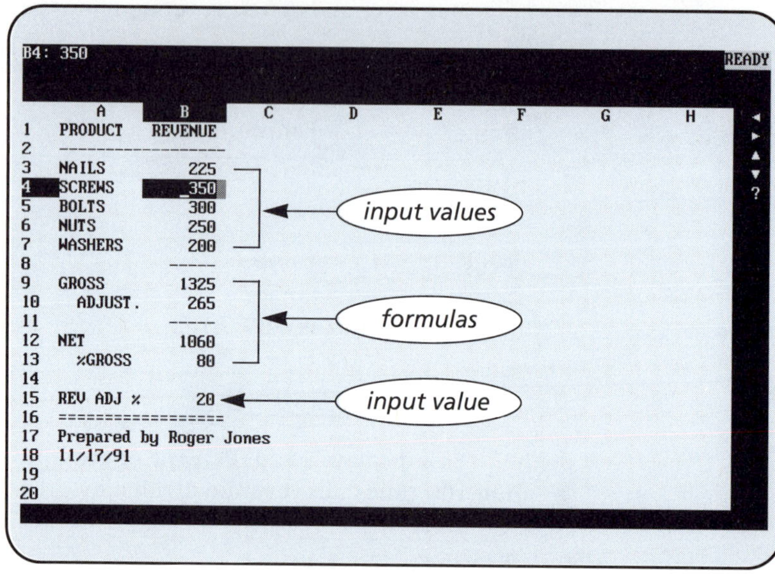

You now print the modified worksheet. Be sure your printer is ready and you are at the top of a page.

Press	/, P, P, A	Selects Print, Printer, Align.

1-2-3 has saved the last selected print range, A1..C18, with the worksheet. The range is listed in the Global Settings display. Selecting the Range option would highlight the range on the screen and give its address in the control panel.

Press	G, P, Q	Selects Go, Page, Quit.

The report is printed, the paper is moved to the top of the next page, and you are returned to Ready mode. You now save the modified worksheet.

Press	/, F, S	Selects File, Save.
Type	REV06	
Press	↵ ENTER	Saves worksheet in REV06.

The current worksheet is saved in the new worksheet file named REV06. You now store the worksheet again using the QTRMAST filename for the template.

Press	/, F, S, ESC	Selects File, Save.

The Escape key displays a list of files from the current directory on the second line of the control panel.

Move to	QTRMAST.WK1	Highlights filename QTRMAST.
Press	↵ ENTER, R	Selects Replace.

The worksheet is saved in the worksheet file named QTRMAST, replacing the previous contents.

PROCEDURE SUMMARY

BUILDING FORMULAS BY POINTING

Move the cell pointer to the cell in which you want to enter the formula.	(pointer-movement keys or mouse)
Type a plus sign to begin the formula.	+
Build the formula using cell addresses, numbers, and symbols.	
Enter cell addresses by highlighting the cell.	(pointer-movement keys or mouse)
Enter numbers by typing.	(your input)
Enter arithmetic operators and parentheses by typing.	(your input)
Enter the formula into the cell.	↵ ENTER

EXERCISES

6A In this exercise, you practice using 1-2-3 as a calculator and you create formulas.

1. In cell B2, add 275 and 708.
2. In cell B3, subtract 89 from 507.
3. In cell B4, multiply 17 times 6 times 8.
4. In cell B5, divide 72 by 7.
5. Print the worksheet.
6. Enter the number 5 in cell A10.
7. Enter the number 10 in cell B10.
8. Enter the number 2 in cell C10.
9. In cell A12, calculate the sum of cells A10, B10, and C10.

10. In cell A13, calculate the sum of cells A10 and B10 and then subtract cell C10 from the sum.
11. In cell A14, multiply cell A10 times cell C10.
12. In cell A15, divide the sum of cells A10 and C10 by cell B10.
13. In cell A16, compute the cube of cell C10.
14. In cell A17, subtract cell A10 from cell B10 and then divide the result by cell C10.
15. In cell A18, determine the square root of cell B10.
16. Print the worksheet.

6B In this exercise, you create a worksheet that includes formulas.

1. Retrieve the E04B file.
2. Center the text "Q2" in cell C2.
3. Enter the text "Assumptions for product growth rates:" in cell A6.
4. Enter the text "Washers" in cell A7 and the text "Dryers" in cell A8.
5. Enter the number 0.03 in cell C7.
6. Enter the number 0.02 in cell C8.
7. In cell C3, enter a formula to increase sales of Washers by 3% over the sales values for Washers in Q1 (Quarter 1). The formula should be sales of Washers in Q1 times (1 plus the growth rate for Washers in Q2). The 1-2-3 formula is +B3*(1+C7).
8. In cell C4, enter a formula to increase sales of Dryers by 2% over the sales value of Dryers in Q1. The formula should be sales for Dryers in Q1 times (1 plus the growth rate for Dryers in Q2). The 1-2-3 formula should be +B4*(1+C8).
9. Save the worksheet using the filename E06B.
10. Print the worksheet.
11. Change the growth rate for Washers in cell C7 to 0.05.
12. Save the worksheet using the filename E06B.
13. Print the worksheet.

Checkpoint 1
What You Should Know

- ✓ The first keystroke typed in a cell determines whether the entry is a label, a number, or a formula.
- ✓ You can move around the worksheet using the pointer-movement keys or a mouse.
- ✓ You can use Lotus 1-2-3 as a calculator.
- ✓ 1-2-3 allows you to enter formulas to calculate values.
- ✓ Text can be left aligned, centered, or right aligned.
- ✓ Values are always right aligned.
- ✓ You can save worksheets in a file for later use.
- ✓ 1-2-3 allows you to print a range of cells from a worksheet or the entire worksheet.

Review Questions

1. Which keys are used to move the cell pointer?
2. What are the methods for creating a formula in 1-2-3?
3. How can you correct errors in a worksheet cell?
4. How do you move the cell pointer using a mouse?
5. How do you start the 1-2-3 program?
6. How do you select commands from 1-2-3 menus?
7. What are the steps for selecting a range by pointing?
8. What are the steps for printing the contents of a worksheet?
9. How do you exit the 1-2-3 program?
10. What are the steps for saving a worksheet to a file?

CHECKPOINT PROBLEM A

The filename convention for Checkpoint problems is different than that for the exercises in each topic. The coding for the filenames is CPxPy, where CP is Checkpoint, x is the Checkpoint number, P is problem, and y is the problem identifier.

1. Create the following worksheet.

		ACME SPORTING GOODS		
DAY	Skis	Boots	Poles	Total
Monday	57	98	124	279
Tuesday	60	25	74	159
Wednesday	104	75	180	359
Thursday	65	45	130	240
Friday	91	67	190	348
Saturday	95	60	175	330
	----------	----------	----------	----------
Total	472	370	873	1715

The worksheet includes sales for several products by day for a sporting goods store. When you create formulas, use the pointing method.

2. Save the worksheet using the filename CP1PA.
3. Print the worksheet.
4. Make sure the worksheet stored in the CP1PA file appears on your screen. Change some of the sales numbers and be sure the total values change correctly.

CHECKPOINT PROBLEM B

1. Create the following worksheet.

		ABC Lumber Company		
	Jan	Feb	Mar	First Qtr
Sales	10000	11000	12100	33100
Expenses	6000	6600	7260	19860
	----------	----------	----------	----------
Gr Profit	4000	4400	4840	13240
Taxes	1600	1760	1936	5296
	----------	----------	----------	----------
Income	2400	2640	2904	7944
	==========	==========	==========	==========
Average Monthly Income				2648
Assumptions for expenses percentage and tax rate				
Expenses	0.6	0.6	0.6	
Tax Rate	0.4	0.4	0.4	

The worksheet includes a projection of monthly income for a lumber company. When you create formulas, use the pointing method.

Use the following assumptions in creating the worksheet:

Sales values are input numbers.

Expenses are calculated by multiplying Sales by 60%.

Gr Profit is determined by subtracting Expenses from Sales.

Taxes are computed by multiplying Gr Profit by 40%.

Income is calculated by subtracting Taxes from Gr Profit.

2. Save the worksheet using the filename CP1PB.
3. Print the worksheet.
4. Make sure the worksheet stored in the CP1PB file is on your screen.
5. Change some sales values, expense rates, and tax rates. Each time check that all the calculated values change correctly.

Editing a Worksheet

CONCEPTS One of the constants of working with worksheets is the need for change. Many worksheets are designed to report the on-going operations of a business and are changed routinely, for example, by entering new information every month. Other applications are designed to forecast the future. The values and relationships in these worksheets are changed to reflect the uncertainties in such a task. In other situations, you may start a new worksheet by modifying an existing one that already contains many of the relationships that you need. You may need to change existing worksheets to reflect changes in operations, organizational structure, or business reporting needs.

In addition to the changes that occur as part of the on-going evolution of your worksheets, you must be able to edit the worksheets as you build them. You need to correct typographical errors. You need to change tentative layouts by moving information around, inserting rows or columns, and abbreviating or extending text.

This topic and Topic 8 discuss the tools that 1-2-3 provides to help you edit and change your worksheet.

Editing Information Without Retyping 85

If a cell contains incorrect information, you can replace it by entering the correct information. However, if the entry is long, it may be easier to **edit** it, correcting only the errors. To edit the contents of a cell, put the cell pointer in the cell and press the F2 function key, called the EDIT key. 1-2-3 places the cell contents on the second line of the control panel and switches to Edit mode. You then make the corrections using the techniques described in this section. Similarly, as you are typing information in the control panel, you can use the BACKSPACE key to erase the last characters and the ESCAPE key to erase the entire entry (Topic 3). Either of these methods may require considerable retyping in a long entry. So, again, it can be quicker to press the EDIT key and use the various editing techniques.

1-2-3 may also place you in Edit mode automatically. For example, if you try to enter an invalid expression for a formula or a value, 1-2-3 beeps and switches to Edit mode to allow you to correct the entry. 1-2-3 also uses Edit mode in commands to accept typed input.

While editing, you use the **edit cursor** to indicate what to change. When you enter Edit mode by pressing the EDIT key, the cursor appears at the end of the entry. If you enter Edit mode due to an error, 1-2-3 places the cursor where it detected the error to try to help you assess the problem.

You move the cursor using the movement keys. As described in Table 7.1, in Edit mode, these keys do not work the same as in Ready mode. The LEFT and RIGHT ARROW keys and the CONTROL-LEFT ARROW and CONTROL-RIGHT ARROW combinations move the cursor 1 or 5 spaces through the text in the indicated direction. The HOME key and END key move the cursor to the beginning and end, respectively, of the entry.

Table 7.1
1-2-3 Editing Keys

Keys	Use
F2 or EDIT	In Ready mode, puts the contents of the current cell on the control panel to edit. Switches between Edit mode and Value or Label mode.
← →	Moves the cursor 1 space in the indicated direction.
CTRL-← CTRL-→	Moves the cursor 5 spaces in the indicated direction.
HOME	Moves the cursor to the beginning of the entry.
END	Moves the cursor to the end of the entry.
ESC	Erases the entry. (Press twice to return to Ready mode.)
←BACKSPACE	Erases the character to the left of the cursor.
DELETE	Erases the character above the cursor.
INSERT	Switches between inserting and overstriking.
↵ENTER	Stores the entry in the cell.
↑ ↓ PAGE UP PAGE DOWN	Stores the entry in the cell and moves as indicated or switches to Point mode.

TIP You can also press the INSERT key which toggles the *OVR* status indicator. When the indicator is on, 1-2-3 overwrites existing text with your input. 1-2-3 returns to the insertion mode when you press the INSERT key again or when you save the entry.

When you have placed the cursor at the point to be corrected, you can type new text and delete existing text. As you type in new text, 1-2-3 inserts your input in front of the character that is above the cursor. The cursor, the character, and the following text slide to the right. ◀

TIP When you are in Edit mode, you cannot initially point to the left or right because these keys move the cursor within the text to be edited. To point in those directions, first press the UP or DOWN ARROW keys to start pointing and then move to the correct location.

TIP When the Undo feature is in effect, the *UNDO* status indicator appears on the status line. You turn the feature on and off using the /Worksheet Global Default Other Undo Enable and Disable commands. It cannot be enabled if there is data in the worksheet.

TIP You gain many of the benefits of the Undo feature just by saving your worksheet prior to making any change that might adversely affect a large portion of it.

To delete text, you can use either the BACKSPACE key or the DELETE key. The BACKSPACE key erases the character to the left of the cursor, whereas the DELETE key erases the character above the cursor. You press either key as many times as necessary to erase the erroneous text.

When you have finished editing the entry, press the ENTER key or any vertical movement key. If the entry is a label, 1-2-3 stores it in the cell and, if appropriate, moves the cell pointer. For values, the process is more involved. If the entry correctly expresses a value, 1-2-3 stores it in the cell. However, suppose the cursor is at the end of the entry and the last character in the entry is a character such as a plus sign, indicating that a cell reference should follow. If you press a vertical movement key, 1-2-3 switches to Point mode, adding the cell pointer location to the end of the formula. You proceed in the normal fashion to complete the formula. ◀

Undoing a Change

1-2-3 provides an optional feature called the **Undo feature** that allows you to reverse the most recent change you have made to your worksheet. You invoke the Undo feature by pressing the key combination ALT-F4, called the UNDO keys, when you are in Ready mode. The worksheet returns to the way it was the last time you were in Ready mode. Pressing the UNDO keys again undoes the undo. ◀

Consider the following examples of the use of the Undo feature. If you retrieve a worksheet file or use the /Worksheet Erase command without saving the previous worksheet, press the UNDO keys and the previous worksheet is restored. If you inadvertently press the SPACEBAR and enter a blank character into a cell that contained a complicated formula, press UNDO and the formula is restored.

1-2-3 implements the Undo feature by taking a complete snap shot of your worksheet as you begin each activity that could change the worksheet. Be careful, however. 1-2-3 takes this snap shot as soon as you press the slash key or begin to enter data into the cell. Thus, if you make a mistake, you must undo it immediately before you start any other commands or data entry operations. The price of the Undo feature is memory. 1-2-3 must set aside a large portion of available memory for use of the Undo feature. For large worksheets this may be a problem. ◀

Erasing a Cell or Range of Cells 85

By editing you can change the contents of a cell, but you cannot completely remove data from the cell. To erase the contents of a cell, you use the /Range Erase command. As with many other 1-2-3 commands, the /Range Erase command acts on ranges of cells. The command is used to erase a single cell, a column or row of cells, or any rectangular block.

To use the /Range Erase command, you normally position the cell pointer in a corner of the range to be erased. Then select the command. 1-2-3 requests the range of cells to be erased, suggesting the range address of the current cell as the response and placing you in Point mode. Press the ENTER key to erase the current cell. You specify any other range beginning with the current cell by expanding the cell pointer. Watch your screen carefully as you do this. When the highlight is covering the cells you want

TIP Prior to executing a command, you can highlight the range of cells on which the command is used. Highlight a range of cells by pressing the F4 key and then using the pointer-movement keys to finish highlighting the range of cells. To highlight a range of cells using a mouse, move the mouse pointer to the initial cell in the range, hold down the mouse button, and then move or drag the mouse pointer to the last cell in the range.

to erase, press the ENTER key. 1-2-3 erases all cells in the highlighted area. The worksheet outside of the highlight remains unchanged. Formulas that refer to erased cells treat them as though they contain zeros. ◀

If you start the /Range Erase command when the cell pointer is not in a corner of the range to be erased, press the ESCAPE key once to convert the range address to a cell address. Then move the cell pointer to a corner of the range, and press the period key to anchor the cell pointer and highlight the range to be erased. When you press the ENTER key, 1-2-3 returns the cell pointer to the cell you were in when you started the command.

Although you usually erase cells because you made an error, this is not the only use of the /Range Erase command. You can often use the same worksheet for many different sets of data. For example, you may be analyzing several different products. Each product has its own information but is analyzed with the same reports and formulas. You can create a worksheet for one product, save it, and then erase all of the input data, leaving the formulas and whatever labels would be appropriate for the other products. Then you save it again under a generic name. Such a worksheet with formulas in place but no numerical values is called a **template**. To use the template for another product, you retrieve it, enter the data for the new product, and print your reports. If there is only one report, 1-2-3 even saves the correct print range for you! To save the information for the new product, save the worksheet under a new name, leaving the template unchanged.

TUTORIAL

In this tutorial, you work on editing skills. You learn how to edit expressions that have already been entered into the worksheet. Then you learn how to erase cell contents. Finally, as an application of these techniques, you create a template. You should have a blank worksheet on the screen.

1 **Edit information.** In this tutorial you use the Undo feature. If the *UNDO* indicator is not on in the status line, you first activate the Undo feature.

Press	/, W, G, D	Selects Worksheet, Global, Default.
Press	O, U, E, Q	Selects Other, Undo, Enable, Quit.

Now retrieve the REV06 worksheet and put the cell pointer in A17.

Press	/, F, R	Selects File, Retrieve.
Type	REV06 ↵ENTER	Retrieves REV06.

You use the F2 function key to enter Edit mode. To practice the various editing techniques, you change the footnote in cell A17 of the REVENUE worksheet five times.

Move to	A17	
Press	F2	Enters Edit mode; mode indicator displays *EDIT*.

The cell contents are on line 2 of the control panel for you to edit. A blinking cursor is at the end of the expression. Add the date to the footnote.

Type	SPACEBAR on 11/17/91	Adds text at the end.
Press	↵ENTER	Enters edited footnote into A17; mode indicator displays *READY*.
Press	F2	Enters Edit mode.

The cell contents are put on the control panel for you to edit. You change the 91 to 1991.

Press	← twice	Moves cursor under 9 in 91.
Type	19	Inserts text.
Press	↵ENTER	Enters changes; returns to Ready mode.

Insert a middle initial in "Roger Jones."

Press	F2, CTRL-← four times, →	Enters Edit mode; moves cursor under the "J" in "Jones".
Type	E. SPACEBAR	Inserts text.
Press	↵ENTER	Enters changed expression.

Change "Roger E. Jones" to "R. E. Jones."

Press	F2, CTRL-← four times, ← three times	Enters Edit mode; moves cursor to the space after "Roger."
Press	←BACKSPACE four times	Erases "oger."
Type	.	Inserts period.
Press	↵ENTER	Enters changed expression.

Change the beginning of the expression to "Figures prepared."

Press	F2, HOME, →	Enters Edit mode; moves to under the "P" in "Prepared."
Press	DELETE	Erases the "P".
Type	Figures p	Inserts text after the apostrophe.

Erase the date from the end of the footnote.

Press	END	Moves to end of phrase.
Press	←BACKSPACE fourteen times	
Press	↵ENTER	Enters changed expression.

You have now used most of the editing techniques. The label in A17 should say "Figures prepared by R. E. Jones". Since the next section uses a different worksheet, you must save your changes.

Press	/, F, S	Selects File, Save.
Type	REV07 ↵ENTER	Saves worksheet under REV07.

TIP Recall that you do not have to erase the current entries. The new data simply replaces the current entries.

2 **Replace entries.** You are going to change the QTRMAST worksheet that you saved in Topic 6. First you create a worksheet, which contains actual revenue numbers for the first quarter (Figure 7.1). Then you create a template (Figure 7.2) from the first quarter worksheet. To begin, you change the heading on the second column, enter new data, and change the way adjustments are handled. ◀

Press	/, F, R	Selects File, Retrieve.
Highlight	QTRMAST.WK1	Chooses the QTRMAST file to retrieve.
Press	↵ENTER	Retrieves QTRMAST.
Move to	B1	

You change the heading from REVENUE to 1ST QTR. The first attempt does not succeed.

Type	1ST QTR	
Press	↵ENTER	1-2-3 beeps; mode indicator displays *EDIT*.

1-2-3 does not store the entry. Since the first character is a number, 1-2-3 expected numeric information. It went into Edit mode with the cursor under the "S," the first problem character in the expression. To enter a label that begins with a number, you must first type a label prefix.

Press	(HOME)	Moves to beginning of phrase.
Type	"	Inserts right alignment label prefix.
Press	(↵ENTER), (↓) twice	Enters 1ST QTR as a right-aligned label; moves to B3.

> **TIP** Note how multiple data entries are presented here. For example, you are to type the number 57, then press the DOWN ARROW key, and so on.

You now enter the product revenue data in column B. Note how the total changes as you enter the new values.

`Type the following numbers pressing the Down Arrow after each number: 57, 80, 72, 64, and 47.` ◀

You are going to change revenue adjustments from a computed percentage of gross revenue to an input value.

Press	(↓) twice	Moves to B10.
Type	60 (↵ENTER)	Enters 60 in B10.

The number 60 replaces the formula in cell B10. Check the current cell contents. The formulas in cells B12 and B13 continue to work properly. They use the value from cell B10 whether it is an input number or a computed result. You now replace the double underlining in A16 with a new footnote.

Press	(↓) six times, (←)	Moves to A16.
Type	Figures prepared by E. P. Michael on 4/10/91	
Press	(→)	Enters footnote; moves to B16.

Only part of the footnote is visible in the worksheet area. It is truncated by the contents of B16.

3 **Erase cells.** To complete the creation of the first quarter worksheet, you erase the rest of the double underlining, the old footnote, and the revenue adjustment percent since revenue adjustment is now an input value. You do this with the /Range Erase command.

Press	(/), (R), (E)	Selects Range, Erase.

The message "Enter range to erase: B16..B16" appears on the second line of the control panel. The mode indicator displays *POINT*. Since you want to erase cell B16, press the Enter key to select this suggested range.

Press	(↵ENTER), (↓), (←)	Erases contents of B16; moves to A17.

The entire footnote in A16 is now visible.

> **TIP** A mouse can be used instead of the pointer-movement keys to highlight the range of cells on which a command is to execute. The range of cells is highlighted by moving the mouse pointer to the initial cell in the range and then dragging the mouse pointer to the last cell.

Press	/, R, E	Selects Range, Erase.

The message "Enter range to erase: A17..A17" is on the control panel. You select the range containing the footnote by pointing.

Press	↓, ↵ ENTER	Erases A17..A18. ◀

The old footnotes are erased. You move up and erase the revenue adjustment percent, including the label.

Press	↑ twice	Moves to A15.
Press	/, R, E	Selects Range, Erase.

The message is "Enter range to erase: A15..A15."

Press	→, ↵ ENTER	Erases A15..B15.

Your worksheet should look like Figure 7.1.

Figure 7.1
1st Quarter Revenue

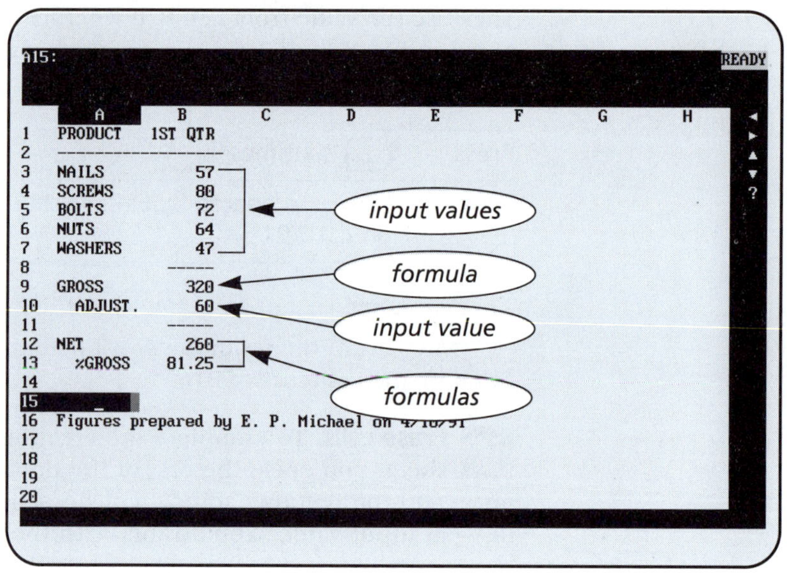

You erase the worksheet before saving it. You use the Undo keys to restore the worksheet.

Press	/, W, E, Y, Y	Selects Worksheet, Erase, Yes.
Press	ALT-F4	Restores worksheet.
Press	/, F, S	Selects File, Save.
Type	QTR1REV ↵ ENTER	Saves worksheet under QTR1REV.

4 **Create a template.** To convert QTR1REV to a template, you change the column heading and erase the numeric input, leaving the labels and formulas.

Move to	B1	

You change the heading to a generic form to be edited when the worksheet is used for a specific quarter.

Type	"XXX QTR	
Press	↓ twice	Enters XXX QTR; moves to B3.

You erase the product revenue values in column B.

Press	/, R, E	Selects Range, Erase.
Press	↓ four times	Highlights revenue values, B3.. B7.
Press	↵ENTER	Erases the range B3..B7.

Note that the total gross revenue is now zero. 1-2-3 recomputes the value displayed in the cell, treating the empty cells as zeros. B13, the percentage of gross revenue, displays ERR for error. The formula in this cell contains a division by B9, the gross revenue. But this value is 0, and division by 0 is undefined. As soon as a nonzero value appears in B9, the computed value displays on the screen in B13.

Move to	B10	
Press	/, R, E	Selects Range, Erase.
Press	↵ENTER	Erases adjustment value, B10.

You replace the specific footnote with a generic footnote.

Move to	A16	
Press	F2	Enters Edit mode.
Press	←BACKSPACE twenty-four times	Erases E. P. Michael on 4/10/91.
Type	---------- on MM/DD/YY	
Press	↵ENTER	Enters edited footnote.

You now select a print range, which will be saved with the worksheet.

Press	/, P, P, R	Selects Print, Printer, Range.

The suggested range is A1..C18. You change it to highlight A1..E16, the contents of the new worksheet.

Press	→ twice, ↑ twice	Highlights the range A1..E16.
Press	↵ ENTER	Locks in range selection.
Press	Q	Selects Quit.

Your worksheet should look like Figure 7.2.

Figure 7.2
Template

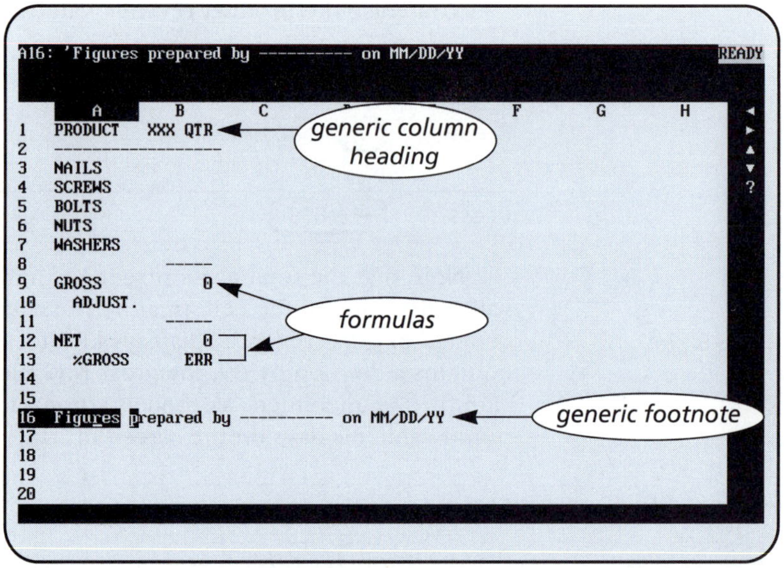

Finally you save the template you have created. When you want to use the template, you retrieve it, enter the data and column heading for the current quarter, and print out the report. Then you save the worksheet under a different appropriate name.

Press	/, F, S, ESC, F3	Selects File, Save, Escape, Name.

You get a full screen display of filenames. You select QTRMAST from this list.

Highlight	QTRMAST.WK1	
Press	↵ ENTER, R	Saves the template.

PROCEDURE SUMMARY

EDITING INFORMATION WITHOUT RETYPING

Move the cell pointer to the cell containing the expression to be edited.	(pointer-movement keys or mouse)
Select Edit mode and bring cell contents to control panel.	F2
Move through the expression.	
Move the cursor to the beginning of the expression.	HOME
Move the cursor to the end of the expression.	END
Move the cursor one character left or right.	← or →
Move the cursor five characters left or right.	CTRL-← or CTRL-→
Erase a character in the expression.	
Delete character to left of cursor.	←BACKSPACE
Delete character above cursor.	DELETE
Enter new characters into the expression.	
Insert new characters to the left of the cursor by typing them.	(your input)
Overwrite characters at the cursor with new characters.	INSERT
Type the new characters.	(your input)
Enter the edited data.	↵ENTER

ERASING A CELL OR RANGE OF CELLS

Move the cell pointer to the upper left corner of the range.	(pointer-movement keys)
Activate the Main menu.	/
Select Range.	R
Select Erase.	E
Highlight the range to erase.	(pointer-movement keys or mouse)
Erase the highlighted range.	↵ENTER

EXERCISES

7A Create a worksheet, save the worksheet to a file, and print the worksheet.

1. Enter the text "Thomas Comcany" in cell A2.
2. Use the EDIT key to spell the word "Company" correctly.
3. Enter the text "Xanuary 2, 1993" in cell A3.
4. Use the edit key to enter the date "January 2, 1991."
5. Enter the number 179 in cell A4.
6. Use the EDIT key to change the number in cell A4 to 379.
7. Enter the text "Item" in cell A6.
8. Enter the text "Quantity" in cell B6.
9. Enter the text "Balls" in cell A7.
10. Enter the number 334 in cell B7.
11. Print the worksheet.
12. Save the worksheet using the filename E07A.
13. Erase the contents of cells A6 and B6.
14. Right align the text "Component" in cell A6.
15. Right align the text "Volume" in cell B6.
16. Save the worksheet using the filename E07A.
17. Print the worksheet.

7B Retrieve an existing worksheet, modify the worksheet, save the changed worksheet, and print the worksheet.

1. Retrieve the E06B file.
2. Use the EDIT key to insert the text "Appliance" after Able in cell A1.
3. Erase cells C7 and C8.
4. Enter the number 0.03 in cell C7 and the number 0.02 in cell C8.
5. Save the worksheet using the filename E07B.
6. Print the worksheet.

Modifying a Worksheet

CONCEPTS

Topic 7 discussed how to change data already stored in cells. In this topic, you investigate how to rearrange data in your worksheet by inserting or deleting rows and columns and moving blocks of cells. These activities are very important in practice. In the development stage of a worksheet, you can try an initial layout and modify it later as you gain more experience. These capabilities also play an important role in the on-going use of the worksheet. For example, you may insert and delete rows to include new products or delete those that no longer are sold.

An important consideration when making such changes is how they impact the calculations in the worksheet. 1-2-3 makes some adjustments automatically. For example, it changes formulas to use the new addresses of moved cells. However, depending on the changes that are made, you may need to modify some formulas to obtain the correct results.

Inserting Rows and Columns

97

To insert rows and columns in the worksheet, you use the /Worksheet Insert Row and /Worksheet Insert Column commands. Prior to using these commands, it is convenient to place the cell pointer where the first new row or column is to go. To insert a new blank row between rows 4 and 5, place the cell pointer anywhere in row 5 since this is where the new row will appear. All the rows from 5 on move down one row. To insert a new column at the beginning of the worksheet, place the cell pointer anywhere in column A, which is where the new column will go.

In the rest of this discussion, we will generally refer to rows. However, all statements apply equally well to columns. To run the command, you select /Worksheet Insert, followed by either Row or Column. 1-2-3 requests the rows to be inserted and places you in Point mode with the range address of the current cell in the control panel. If you want to insert only one row, you press the ENTER key. To insert multiple rows, press the DOWN ARROW key to highlight the location of the new rows and then press the ENTER key. If the cell pointer is not where the first row is to be inserted, press the ESCAPE key to convert the range address to a cell address. Then move to the first row and anchor the cell pointer. ◀

> **TIP** Since 1-2-3 automatically highlights the first row for you, press the DOWN ARROW key one time fewer than the number of rows to be inserted. Note that you only have to highlight one cell in each row.

All cells in the new rows will be empty. In addition, formulas that referred to cells that moved will be modified to refer to the new locations. For example, suppose we insert a new row between rows 4 and 5. Any formula that referred to a cell in row 5, for example, B5, now refers to the new location of the cell in row 6, that is, B6. This means that all previous formulas continue to give the correct result. ◀

Once you enter new data in the inserted cells, some formulas may no longer be correct. For example, suppose you enter a new salesperson into a worksheet that computes commissions. Formulas in the worksheet may then need to be changed to properly include the new salesperson. Also, other parts of the worksheet may need similar insertions. Some of the required changes can be simplified by properly designing your worksheets (Topic 12). In general, however, modifying worksheets requires careful attention. In practice, incorrect or incomplete changes to previously correct worksheets are a major source of errors. ◀

In addition to adjusting formulas for inserted rows, 1-2-3 adjusts remembered ranges in commands. For example, if the print range was A1..H10, inserting a new row at row 5 changes the range to A1..H11. Any data placed in row 5 will be included in your report. However, insertions before or after the print range will not be included in the existing range. For example, inserting two new columns at the beginning of the worksheet changes the print range from A1..H10 to C1..J10. This range covers the same cells as before but in their new location. Any data placed in the new columns A and B will not be included in the range.

TIP: If you insert rows erroneously, you can use the /Worksheet Delete Row command to remove them, or you can use the Undo feature if it is active.

TIP: When a group first uses 1-2-3, most of its efforts go into developing new worksheets. But, eventually, much more time is spent on *maintaining* existing worksheets. Do not underestimate the importance of or the time involved in this activity.

TIP: Notice the difference between deleting and erasing. Erasing removes the data from the cells but leaves the cells. So, although formulas that refer to the erased cells treat their contents as zeros, the formulas are not changed.

Deleting Rows and Columns

97

To delete adjacent rows and columns from the worksheet, you use the /Worksheet Delete Row and /Worksheet Delete Column commands. After selecting either command, you indicate the rows or columns to be deleted by pointing and then press the ENTER key.

1-2-3 deletes the highlighted rows and automatically adjusts formulas and remembered ranges. The only difficulty occurs if a formula in the worksheet refers to a cell that was deleted. In this case, the cell reference in the formula is replaced by the word "ERR," and the cell displays the value ERR in the worksheet area. The formula is invalid and must be edited or replaced. Thus, if you delete row 5 in the worksheet, the formula 0.07*B5 is replaced by 0.07*ERR. Furthermore, any other formula that refers to the cell containing the invalid formula also displays ERR in the worksheet area since one of its inputs is erroneous. ◀

Since you can see only a portion of your worksheet at any one time, you should examine the rows you are going to delete along their entire length before deleting them. If there are errors in your worksheet after you make the deletions, you can use the Undo feature to reverse the last deletions.

If you delete rows from the middle of or in front of a remembered range, such as a print range, 1-2-3 automatically readjusts the range to cover the remaining cells in their new locations. The only exception is if you delete a row containing a corner of the range. 1-2-3 then regards the remembered range as undefined, and you must redefine it the next time you use the command.

Moving Information

(97)

The /Move command moves information from one range of cells, the **Move what? range**, into another, the **To where? range**. Both of these ranges have the same shape but different locations. When you use the /Move command, 1-2-3 first asks you to specify the Move what? range. The mode indicator displays *POINT*, and the *range* address of the current cell is the suggested response. You specify the Move what? range by highlighting it and pressing the ENTER key. 1-2-3 then requests the To where? range. Once again the mode indicator displays *POINT* but with the *cell* address of the current cell as the suggested response. This makes it easy to move to the To where? range. You only need to point to the upper left corner of the To where? range and press ENTER.

1-2-3 moves the contents of the Move what? range and places them so that the upper left corner is located at the To where? cell. If the Move what? and To where? ranges do not overlap, the cells in the Move what? range will all be empty. Anything that was in cells in the To where? range is replaced by the data from the corresponding cell in the Move what? range. This is true even if the cell in the Move what? range was empty.

As it moves the cells, 1-2-3 also adjusts formulas in the worksheet. Any formula that refers to a cell in the Move what? range is adjusted to refer to the new location of the cell. This includes formulas both inside and outside of the Move what? range. However, if a formula referred to a cell in the To where? range that was replaced by the data from the Move what? range, the cell reference in the formula is replaced by ERR and the cell containing the formula displays ERR as its result.

Ranges are adjusted depending on how their corners are affected by the move. For example, if cell H10 is moved to cell G15, the range A1..H10 is converted to the range A1..G15, assuming cell A1 was not moved. However, if the corner of a range lies in the To where? range and is replaced by the Move what? range, 1-2-3 treats the remembered range as undefined. You must redefine the range. ◀

TIP You can use the /Move command to insert rows across only a portion of the worksheet since this is equivalent to moving a portion of the worksheet down. When you highlight the Move what? range, be sure that you include all the data below the new row's intended location.

TUTORIAL In this tutorial, you modify the REV07 worksheet by adding a new column, alphabetizing the products, and adding new products. The new techniques used are inserting and deleting rows and columns and moving cell contents around in a worksheet. In addition, you practice such old skills as moving around the worksheet, entering labels and numbers, and, most important, entering and editing formulas. The REV07 worksheet should be on the screen.

1 **Insert a row and a column.** In this section, you insert a new row for additional headings at the top of the worksheet. You insert a new second column for prior year revenues.

Move to	B1

The cell pointer can be anywhere in row 1 to insert a new row at the top of the worksheet.

Press	/, W, I, R	Selects Worksheet, Insert, Row.

The message "Enter row insert range: B1..B1" is on the control panel. Here you are inserting only one row, so you press ENTER.

Press	↵ ENTER	Inserts a new row at top of worksheet.
Move to	B10	Moves to new location of the total formula.

Check the formula in the control panel. 1-2-3 has changed the cell references to correspond to the new location of the revenue values. For example, the value that was originally in B3 is now in B4, and the cell reference to B3 in the formula has become B4 in the moved formula. You insert a new column B to contain prior year revenues.

Press	/, W, I, C	Selects Worksheet, Insert, Column.

The message "Enter column insert range: B10..B10" appears.

Press	↵ ENTER	Inserts a new column B.

There is a blank column between columns A and C. The information that was in column B has moved to column C. Again look at the impact that moving has on the cell contents, particularly on the formulas, in what is now column C. Where there were cell addresses from column B, there are now addresses from column C.

2 **Fill in the new column.** Next you input information into the new cells starting with the column headings.

Move to	B1	
Press	CAPS LOCK	Turns on *CAPS* indicator.
Type	"PRIOR	
Press	→	Inputs "PRIOR" right aligned in B1; moves to C1.
Type	"PLAN	
Press	↓, ←	Enters "PLAN" right aligned; moves to B2.
Type	"REVENUE	

Press	↓	Enters REVENUE; moves to B3.
Type	\-	
Press	↓	Underlines column heading; moves to B4.

Enter the prior year revenue values down column B.

```
Enter the following numbers pressing the Down
Arrow after each number: 200, 325, 268, 222, and 210.
```

Type	"_____	
Press	↓	Underlines column of numbers; moves to B10.

Now you build the appropriate formulas using the pointing technique, that is, by typing in the operations and numbers and by highlighting the cells. You start with the formula for total gross revenue. The details are left to you.

Build	+B4+B5+B6+B7+B8	
Press	↵ ENTER, ↓	Enters gross revenue formula; moves to B11.

Note that when you are building a formula by pointing, the Down Arrow does not enter the formula into the cell. It changes the cell to which you are pointing. You now enter the adjustments for the prior year, which are known and can be entered as values.

Type	302 ↓	Enters revenue adjustments; moves to B12.
Type	"_____	
Press	↓	Underlines; moves to B13.

You now enter formulas for net revenue and percent of gross revenue.

Build	+B10-B11	
Press	↵ ENTER, ↓	Enters net revenue formula; moves to B14.
Build	+100*B13/B10	
Press	↵ ENTER, ↓ three times	Enters percent of gross revenue formula; moves to B17.

Note that the display of the percent of gross revenue value in B14 is hard to read. This problem is handled in Topic 10. Finally you fill the gap in the double underlining in row 17.

Type	\=	
Press	↵ ENTER	Fills B17 with double underlining.

3 **Enter a worksheet heading.** You insert three new rows and add a heading at the top of the worksheet.

Press	HOME	Moves to A1.
Press	/, W, I, R	Selects Worksheet, Insert, Row.

The message "Enter row insert range: A1..A1" is on the control panel.

Press	↓ twice	Highlights three rows via the range A1..A3.
Press	↵ ENTER	Inserts three new rows.
Press	SPACEBAR three times, ACE HARDWARE	
Press	↓	Enters " ACE HARDWARE"; moves to A2.
Type	'1991 REVENUE FORECAST	
Press	↵ ENTER	Enters label into A2.

Your worksheet should look like Figure 8.1.

Figure 8.1
Revenue Worksheet with New Rows and Column

```
   ACE HARDWARE
1991 REVENUE FORECAST

                  PRIOR     PLAN
PRODUCT         REVENUE  REVENUE
-------------------------------
NAILS               200      225
SCREWS              325      350
BOLTS               268      300
NUTS                222      250
WASHERS             210      200
                  -----    -----
GROSS              1225     1325
  ADJUST.           302      265
                  -----    -----
NET                 923     1060
  % GROSS 75.34693            80

REV ADJ %                     20
===============================
Figures prepared by R. E. Jones
11/17/91
```

4 **Move product information.** You now use row insertion and deletion with the /Move command to alphabetize the product names. In Topic 15, you will learn how to sort using the /Data Sort command. BOLTS should be the first row.

Move to	A7	
Press	/, W, I, R	Selects Worksheet, Insert, Row.
Press	↵ENTER	Inserts a new row 7 for BOLTS.
Move to	A10	
Press	/	Activates the Main menu.
Press	M	Selects Move; mode indicator displays *POINT*.

The message "Move what? A10..A10" is on the control panel. You point to the information you want moved.

Press	→ twice	Highlights BOLTS row.

Message is now "Move what? A10..C10."

Press	↵ENTER	Locks in selection.

The message "To where? A10" is on the control panel. Note that the response is presented as a cell address. You highlight the first cell of the To where? range.

Press	↑ three times	Moves to first cell in new row, A7.

The message is now "To where? A7."

Press	↵ENTER	Moves BOLTS row from A10..C10 to A7..C7.

Note the impact of inserting the row and moving the revenue information for BOLTS on the gross revenue formulas at the bottom of the worksheet. You should check them after each step, and we will take a detailed look when all the rearranging is completed. Now you insert a new row 9 for the NUTS data.

Move to	A9	
Press	/, W, I, R	Selects Worksheet, Insert, Row.
Press	↵ENTER	Inserts a new row 9.

You move the NUTS data from row 12 to row 9. This time you start with the cell pointer in A9, the start of the To where? range.

Press	/, M	Selects Move.

The message is "Move what? A9..A9." You now convert the range address to a cell address and move to row 12 to pick the Move what? range.

Press	ESC	Converts A9..A9 to A9.
Press	↓ three times, ., → twice	Selects NUTS row, A12..C12, as Move what? range.
Press	↵ ENTER	Locks in selection and returns cell pointer to A9.

The message is "To where? A9."

Press	↵ ENTER	Moves NUTS row from A12..C12 to A9..C9.

Now delete the rows from which the data was moved.

Move to	A11	
Press	/, W, D, R	Selects Worksheet, Delete, Row.
Press	↓	Highlights both blank rows A11..A12.
Press	↵ ENTER	Deletes rows 11 and 12.

The product names are now arranged alphabetically. Each has had its revenues values moved along with it.

Move to	B13

Look at the total formula in the current cell contents. The cell references have been changed and reflect the new addresses of the original rows.

TIP To specify the location for inserting a row(s), you can highlight a cell in each row(s) prior to using the Worksheet Insert Row command or when you are prompted to enter the row insert range.

5 **Insert new products.** You now insert two new rows in order to include two new products at the bottom of the table. You then must change the total formulas. ◀

Move to	A12	
Press	/, W, I, R	Selects Worksheet, Insert, Row.
Press	↓, ↵ ENTER	Inserts new rows 12 and 13.

Type	HINGES (↓)	Enters HINGES in A12; moves to A13.
Type	BRACKETS (→), (↑)	Enters BRACKETS; moves to B12.

You now enter prior and plan revenue for HINGES and BRACKETS.

Type	10 (↓)
Type	20 (→), (↑)
Type	30 (↓)
Type	50 (↵ ENTER)

Note that the formulas are not correct in cells B15 and C15. Although the formulas do follow cells as they move, they do not include new cells. Topic 12 shows you how to handle such changes automatically. Here you edit the formulas to include the new products.

Move to	B15	
Press	(F2)	Enters Edit mode.
Type	+	
Press	(↑) three times	Points to HINGES prior revenue, B12.
Type	+	Returns cell pointer to B15.
Press	(↑) twice	Points to BRACKETS prior revenue, B13.
Press	(↵ ENTER)	Enters edited formula into B15.

The formula in B15 is now +B8+B10+B7+B9+B11+B12+B13. The value, 1255, displayed in the cell is correct. You now make the same changes to cell C15. In Topic 9, you learn how to do this quickly and accurately using the /Copy command.

Press	(→), (F2)	Moves to C15; enters Edit mode.
Press	(+), (↑) three times	Points to HINGES plan revenue, C12.
Press	(+), (↑) twice	Points to BRACKETS plan revenue, C13.
Press	(↵ ENTER)	Enters edited formula into C15.

C15 displays 1405. You now print the modified worksheet.

Press	/ , P , P , R	Selects Print, Printer, Range.

The print range is now A5..D24. The new rows at the top have not been included, but the rows and column inserted in the middle were. You now change the print range so that it includes the entire worksheet.

Press	ESC	Changes range address to a cell address, A5.
Press	HOME , .	Anchors cell pointer in A1.
Press	PAGE DOWN , ↓ three times, → three times	Expands cell pointer to D24.

The new print range is now A1..D24.

Press	↵ ENTER	Locks in print range.
Press	G , P , Q	Selects Go, Page, Quit.

Prints the report, advances to the next page, and exits the Print menu

Press	CAPS LOCK	Turns off *CAPS* indicator.

Your worksheet should look like Figure 8.2.

Figure 8.2
Revenue Worksheet with New Products

```
  ACE HARDWARE
1991 REVENUE FORECAST

                  PRIOR     PLAN
PRODUCT         REVENUE  REVENUE
--------------------------------
BOLTS               268      300
NAILS               200      225
NUTS                222      250
SCREWS              325      350
WASHERS             210      200
HINGES               10       30
BRACKETS             20       50
                  -----    -----
GROSS              1255     1405
  ADJUST.           302      281
                  -----    -----
NET                 953     1124
  % GROSS  75.93625           80

REV ADJ %                     20
================================
Figures prepared by R. E. Jones
11/17/91
```

Finally, as always, you save the modified worksheet.

Press	/, F, S	Selects File, Save.
Type	REV08 ↵ ENTER	Saves worksheet under REV08.

PROCEDURE SUMMARY

INSERTING ROWS AND COLUMNS

Move the cell pointer to the row or column where the new row(s) or column(s) are to appear.	(pointer-movement keys or mouse)
Activate the Main menu.	/
Select Worksheet.	W
Select Insert.	I
Select Row or Column.	R or C
Highlight a cell in each of the rows or columns to be inserted.	(arrow keys or mouse)
Insert the rows or columns.	↵ ENTER

DELETING ROWS AND COLUMNS

Move the cell pointer to the row or column where the rows or columns are to be deleted.	(pointer-movement keys or mouse)
Activate the Main menu.	/
Select Worksheet.	W
Select Delete.	D
Select Row or Column.	R or C
Highlight a cell in each of the rows or columns to be deleted.	(arrow keys or mouse)
Delete the rows or columns.	↵ ENTER

MOVING INFORMATION

Move the cell pointer to the upper left corner of the Move what? range.	(pointer-movement keys or mouse)
Activate the Main menu.	/

Select Move.	M
Highlight the Move what? range.	(pointer-movement keys or mouse)
Lock in the selection.	↵ ENTER
Move the cell pointer to the upper left corner of the To where? range.	(pointer-movement keys or mouse)
Move the information.	↵ ENTER

EXERCISES

8A Modify an existing worksheet by inserting and deleting rows and columns. Move data from one location on a worksheet to another location.

1. Retrieve the E07A file.
2. Delete row 4.
3. Insert a column at column B in the worksheet.
4. Right align the text "Item No" in cell B5.
5. Right align the text "BA756" in cell B6.
6. Move the contents of cells A2 and A3 to cells B2 and B3.
7. Insert a row at row 2 and insert a column at column A.
8. Move the contents of cells B3 through D7 to cells E1 through G5.
9. Delete columns A, B, and C.
10. Save the worksheet using the filename E08A.
11. Print the worksheet.

8B Modify an existing worksheet by inserting and deleting rows and moving data to another worksheet location.

1. Retrieve the E07B file.
2. Insert six rows at row 2.
3. Enter the text "Sales Forecast" in cell A2 and the text "($000)" in cell A3.
4. Edit the contents of cells A2 and A3 until the text appears to be centered under the contents of cell A1.
5. Move the contents of cells A1 through A3 to cells C1 through C3.
6. Delete rows 5 and 6.
7. Save the worksheet using the filename E08B.
8. Print the worksheet.

Copying

CONCEPTS

One of the most important 1-2-3 commands is the /Copy command. This command and the pointing methods introduced in Topics 5 and 6 form the basic technologies for building worksheets.

Even though a worksheet may be very large and contain hundreds of cells with formulas and data, it will usually contain patterns that you can use to speed its construction. For example, you might want to underline each column in the worksheet and have a total of the column entries at the bottom of the column. Instead of typing the underlines and total formulas in each column, you can enter them in the first column and then use the /Copy command to duplicate them under the other columns.

> **TIP** Sometimes while working in one area of the worksheet, you may want to copy data there from another area. It may be convenient to start the /Copy command in the To where? range because you are already there. When the command has finished executing, 1-2-3 automatically returns you to the same cell.

Copying Data

108

As was the case with the /Move command, the /Copy command requires two ranges, the **Copy what?** range and then the **To where?** range.

You will frequently start the /Copy command in the corner of the Copy what? range. In anticipation of this, 1-2-3 suggests the *range* address of the current cell as the Copy what? range. You then highlight the range to be copied and press the ENTER key.

The initial suggestion for the To where? range is the *cell* address of the current cell. This allows you to move easily to the beginning of the To where? range even if it is in another section of the worksheet. After anchoring the cell pointer, you highlight the cells that will specify the To where? range and press the ENTER key. 1-2-3 copies the data in the Copy what? range into the cells specified by the To where? range. Labels and numerical values are copied exactly; formulas may be adjusted during the copy as described in the next section. ◄

The relationships among the Copy what? range, the To where? range, and the cells into which the data is copied are shown in Table 9.1. The ranges you highlight are enclosed in double lines. The range into which data is copied is shaded. If the Copy what? range is a single cell, the To where? range can be any rectangle. The single cell is copied to fill the rectangle. If the Copy what? range is a single column, the To where? range is specified by the row where the first cell in the Copy what? range is to be copied. The rest of the cells in the Copy what? range will be placed below this row. When the Copy what? range is a rectangle, the upper left corner of the To where? range determines the To where? range.

Table 9.1 *The Relationship Between the Copy what? and To where? ranges*

Copy what? range - Cell

1			

To where? range and Result

1	1	1
1	1	1
1	1	1

Copy what? range - Column

1
2
3

To where? range and Result

1	1	1	1
2	2	2	2
3	3	3	3

Copy what? range - Row

1	2	3	4

To where? range and Result

1	2	3	4
1	2	3	4
1	2	3	4

Copy what? range - Rectangle

1	2	3	4
5	6	7	8

To where? range and Result

1	2	3	4
5	6	7	8

Any data that was previously in the cells into which 1-2-3 copies data is replaced. Formulas that referred to these cells are unchanged, but they now use the new data in the cells. The Copy what? range is not affected by the copy. Note the difference between this behavior and that of the /Move command in which the Copy what? range and other formulas are impacted and can even be destroyed.

Copying Formulas

When 1-2-3 copies formulas, it can adjust the cells the formulas reference. It is very unusual for a worksheet to have the same formula in more than one cell since the same formula always produces the same answer. However, it is very common for worksheets to have similar formulas in different cells. For example, suppose cell B5 has the formula +B2+B3+B4,

> **TIP** Alternatively you can think of 1-2-3 as changing the rows and columns that the formulas reference. For example, for every column to the right or left that the formula is copied, 1-2-3 increases or decreases the columns referred to in the formula by 1.

which sums values in column B. If column C contains data in the same rows, the appropriate summation formula in cell C5 is +C2+C3+C4. When the formula is copied from cell B5 into cell C5, 1-2-3 automatically adjusts the formula to refer to the data in column C. Similarly, if the formula is copied to column D, the cell references will refer to the data in column D.

How does this work? When 1-2-3 refers to cell B2 in a formula in cell B5, it thinks of B2 not in terms of its actual cell address but in terms of its position relative to the cell the formula is in. Thus B2 would be thought of as the cell three rows above in the same column as the cell containing the formula. Cell references written in this way are referred to as **relative references**. Similarly B3 is the cell two rows above and B4 is the cell one row above in the same column. Thought of in this way, the formulas +C2+C3+C4 in cell C5 and +B2+B3+B4 in cell B5 both say "sum the data in the three cells above the cell containing the formula." Thus, copying the formula requires no change at all. ◀

In other instances, it is necessary to deal with specific row or column locations. Such references, called absolute references, are discussed in Topic 12.

Related Commands

A command that is related to the /Copy command is the /Range Value command, which copies the values in a range of cells into another range. Specifically, if the Copy what? range contains formulas, the To where? range will contain the numbers computed from the formulas not the formulas themselves. You can use this command to convert formulas into values by making the Copy what? range and the To where? range coincide. For example, in a worksheet that tracks expenses, you may have rows containing data and calculations. Once input, the data is not changed, and the computed values in each row do not change either. Since formulas take time to recalculate and require much more memory than values, you can use the /Range Value command to replace the formulas in the row by their values.

TUTORIAL

In this tutorial, you learn how to copy cell contents. The advantages to using the /Copy command in building worksheets are an increase in speed and a decrease in errors. You first copy labels. Then you copy formulas and analyze how 1-2-3 adjusts the cell references in the formulas. These techniques are used to add two new columns and a new product to the REV08 worksheet. To begin this tutorial, you should have the REV08 worksheet on the screen.

1 **Copy labels.** When you copy labels (and numbers), the contents of the Copy what? range are simply reproduced in the To where? range. You now enter column headings and underlinings for the Change and Percent Change columns. These columns are added to the right of the current columns.

Move to	E4	
Type	^%	
Press	↓	Enters % centered in E4; moves to E5.
Type	"CHANGE	
Press	↵ ENTER	Enters CHANGE in E5.

You now copy the label in E5 to D5.

Press	/, C	Selects Copy.

The message "Copy what? E5..E5" is on the control panel. The suggested response to the prompt is the current cell presented as a range. This is the range you want.

Press	↵ ENTER	Locks in selection.

The message "To where? E5" is on the control panel. The suggested response to the prompt is the current cell presented as a cell. You point to the range you want as the To where? range.

Press	←, ↵ ENTER	Copies right-aligned CHANGE from E5 to D5.

You do not need to anchor the cell pointer since the To where? range is a single cell. After copying, the cell pointer is in the cell that was current when you started the Copy process. Now you copy the underlining from the Plan Revenue column to the two new columns.

Press	↓, ← twice	Moves to C6.
Press	/, C	Selects Copy.

The suggested Copy what? range is C6..C6.

Press	↵ ENTER	Locks in selection.
Press	→	Highlights first cell in To where? range, D6.
Press	.	Anchors the cell pointer.
Press	→	Highlights To where? range, D6..E6.
Press	↵ ENTER	Copies underlining from C6 to D6..E6.

Repeat the steps of copying the underlining and double underlining in rows 14, 17, and 22.

Press	↓ eight times	Moves to C14.
Press	/, C	Selects Copy.
Press	↵ENTER	Chooses Copy what? range C14..C14.
Press	→	Moves to D14.
Press	., →	Selects To where? range D14..E14.
Press	↵ENTER	Copies from C14 to D14..E14.
Press	↓ three times	Moves to C17.
Press	/, C, ↵ENTER	Selects Copy with Copy what? range C17.
Press	→, ., →	Chooses To where? range D17..E17.
Press	↵ENTER	Copies from C17 to D17..E17.

For the next copy, you use two cells as the Copy what? range and so need only one cell to specify the To where? range.

Press	↓ five times, ←	Moves to B22.
Press	/, C, →, ↵ENTER	Selects Copy what? range B22..C22.
Press	→ twice, ↵ENTER	Copies from B22..C22 to D22..E22.

2 **Enter and copy the change formulas.** In this section, you enter a formula to compute the change in revenue from the prior year to the plan year in cell D7. You then copy this formula to the other rows. You should pay attention to the cell pointer movement techniques, particularly those using the End key.

Move to	D7	
Press	+, ←	Points to plan revenue for BOLTS, C7.
Press	-, ← twice	Points to prior revenue for BOLTS, B7.
Press	↵ENTER	Enters formula into D7.

In the worksheet area D7 displays 32. Now copy the change formula from BOLTS, D7, to the other products, D8..D13.

Press	/, C, ↵ ENTER	Selects Copy with Copy what? range D7.
Press	↓, .	Anchors cell pointer with To where? range D8..D8.
Press	END, ↓	Highlights range D8..D14.

The End key followed by the Down Arrow highlights through the first nonempty cell, D14, after the string of empty cells. This is the desired To where? range, plus an extra cell, which you eliminate.

Press	↑	Excludes underlining.

The Up Arrow changes the highlighted range to include only the remaining products, D8..D13.

Press	↵ ENTER, ↓	Copies formula from D7 to D8..D13; moves to D8.

The formula in the current cell contents reads +C8-B8. The formula has been modified in copying it from D7, but it expresses the same relationship from the point of view of D8. The relationship reads: subtract the value in the cell two cells to the left from the value in the cell to the left. You now copy the Change formula from BOLTS, D7, to gross revenue and adjustments, D15..D16, and then to net revenue and percent of gross, D18..D19.

Press	↑	Moves to D7.
Press	/, C, ↵ ENTER	Selects Copy with Copy what? range D7.
Press	END, ↓ twice	Moves to D15.
Press	., ↓, ↵ ENTER	Copies formula from D7 to D15..D16.
Press	/, C, ↵ ENTER	Selects Copy with Copy what? range D7.
Press	END, ↓ twice	Moves to D18.
Press	., ↓, ↵ ENTER	Copies formula from D7 to D18..D19.

Your worksheet should now look like Figure 9.1.

Figure 9.1

Revenue Worksheet with Change Column

```
   ACE HARDWARE
1991 REVENUE FORECAST

                     PRIOR      PLAN                  %
PRODUCT            REVENUE   REVENUE     CHANGE  CHANGE
-------------------------------------------------------
BOLTS                  268       300         32
NAILS                  200       225         25
NUTS                   222       250         28
SCREWS                 325       350         25
WASHERS                210       200        -10
HINGES                  10        30         20
BRACKETS                20        50         30
                     -----     -----      -----   -----
GROSS                 1255      1405        150
  ADJUST.              302       281        -21
                     -----     -----      -----   -----
NET                    953      1124        171
  % GROSS 75.93625        80 4.063745

REV ADJ %                         20
=======================================================
Figures prepared by R. E. Jones
11/17/91
```

3 Enter and copy the percent change formulas. You now enter the formula for percent change in E7 and copy it to the rest of the rows. The formula for percent change is 100 times the change in revenue divided by the prior year revenue. As usual, you build the formula by pointing, that is, by typing the numbers and characters and by pointing to the cell addresses. The approach that we take to moving the cell pointer is a bit different from the last section.

Press	→	Moves to E7.
Build	100*D7/B7	Uses pointing.
Press	↵ENTER	Enters formula into E7.
Press	/, C, ↵ENTER	Selects Copy with Copy what? range E7.
Press	↓, .	Anchors cell pointer in E8.
Press	END, ↓, END, ↓ three times	Highlights rest of column as To where? range, E8..E19.
Press	↵ENTER	Copies formula from E7 to E8..E19.

Note that the underlinings in cells E14 and E17 have been replaced by ERR. However, it is easy to reenter them either directly or by using the /Copy command. You use the /Copy command here for practice.

Move to	D14	
Press	/, C, ↵ENTER	Selects Copy with Copy what? range D14.
Press	→, ↵ENTER	Copies from D14 to E14.
Press	↓ three times, /, C, ↵ENTER	Moves to E17; selects Copy with Copy what? range E17.
Press	→, ↵ENTER	Copies from D17 to E17.

The underlinings have been reentered.

4 **Copy formulas to add a new row.** You insert a new product at the end of the product list, input its revenue data, and copy the change formulas. As before, you then must adjust the sum formulas at the bottom of the revenue columns.

Move to	A14	
Press	/, W, I, R, ↵ENTER	Selects Worksheet, Insert, Row; inserts a new row 14.
Type	MISCELLANEOUS	
Press	→	Enters label in A14; moves to B14.

Note that the long label MISCELLANEOUS appears to be in B14 also.

Type	12 →	Enters 12 in B14; moves to C14.

As soon as you enter a number in B14, the label in A14 is truncated on the screen. However, the entire label is still in A14, as you will see in Topic 10 when you change column widths.

Type	18 →, ↑	Enters 18 in C14; moves to D13.

You copy the formulas from revenue for BRACKETS, D13..E13, to revenue for MISCELLANEOUS, D14..E14. Here, to specify the To where? range, you only need the first cell in the row.

Press	/, C, →, ↵ENTER	Selects Copy with Copy what? range D13..E13.
Press	↓, ↵ENTER	Copies formulas from D13..E13 to D14..E14.

Include MISCELLANEOUS prior revenue, B14, in the total formula in cell B16 and copy the formula to C16.

Move to	B16	
Press	(F2)	Enters Edit mode.
Press	(+), (↑) twice	Points to prior revenue for MISCELLANEOUS.
Press	(↵ ENTER)	Enters corrected formula in B16.
Press	(/), (C), (↵ ENTER), (→), (↵ ENTER)	Selects Copy, Copy what? and To where? ranges.

The formula is copied from B16 to C16. Your worksheet should look like Figure 9.2.

Figure 9.2

Revenue Worksheet with Percent Change Column

```
  ACE HARDWARE
1991 REVENUE FORECAST

                 PRIOR     PLAN                 %
PRODUCT        REVENUE  REVENUE     CHANGE    CHANGE
---------------------------------------------
BOLTS              268      300         32 11.94029

NAILS              200      225         25      12.5

NUTS               222      250         28 12.61261

SCREWS             325      350         25 7.692307

WASHERS            210      200        -10 -4.76190

HINGES              10       30         20       200

BRACKETS            20       50         30       150

MISCELLAN           12       18          6        50

                 -----    -----      -----    -----

GROSS             1267     1423        156 12.31254

  ADJUST.          302    284.6      -17.4 -5.76158

                 -----    -----      -----    -----

NET                965   1138.4      173.4 17.96891

  % GROSS 76.16416           80   3.835832 5.036269

REV ADJ %                    20
=============================================
Figures prepared by R. E. Jones
11/17/91
```

You now print the new worksheet. The print range is now A1..D25, which includes the new row 14 that was inserted into the middle of the range but does not include column E. You adjust the range.

Press	/, P, P, A	Selects Print, Printer, Align.
Press	R, →, ↵ ENTER	Selects Range with new range A1..E25.
Press	G, P, Q	Selects Go, Page, Quit.

Now you save the modified worksheet.

Press	/, F, S	Selects File, Save.
Type	REV09 ↵ ENTER	Saves the worksheet under REV09.

PROCEDURE SUMMARY

COPYING INFORMATION

To copy the current cell:

Activate the Main menu.	/
Select Copy.	C
Select the current cell as the Copy what? range.	↵ ENTER
Move the cell pointer to the upper left corner of the To where? range.	(pointer-movement keys or mouse)
Anchor the cell pointer.	.
Highlight the range.	(pointer-movement keys or mouse)
Copy the data from the single cell to the To where? range.	↵ ENTER

To copy a row or column of cells:

Move the cell pointer to the beginning of the row or column of cells to be copied.	(pointer-movement keys or mouse)
Activate the Main menu.	/
Select Copy.	C
Highlight the row or column.	(pointer-movement keys or mouse)
Lock in the selection.	↵ ENTER

Move the cell pointer to the upper left corner of the To where? range.	(pointer-movement keys or mouse)
Anchor the cell pointer.	.
Highlight the left column or top row of the To where? range.	(pointer-movement keys or mouse)
Copy the data from the single row or column to the To where? range.	↵ ENTER

To copy a multirow, multicolumn range of cells:

Move the cell pointer to the upper left corner of the Copy what? range.	(pointer-movement keys or mouse)
Activate the Main menu.	/
Select Copy.	C
Highlight the range.	(pointer-movement keys or mouse)
Lock in the selection.	↵ ENTER
Move the cell pointer to the upper left corner of the To where? range.	(pointer-movement keys or mouse)
Copy the data from the Copy what? range to the To where? range.	↵ ENTER

To convert formulas to values:

Move the cell pointer to the upper left corner of the Copy what? range.	(pointer-movement keys or mouse)
Activate the Main menu.	/
Select Range.	R
Select Value.	V
Highlight the Copy what? range.	(pointer-movement keys or mouse)
Lock in the selection.	↵ ENTER
Move the cell pointer to the upper left corner of the To where? range.	(pointer-movement keys or mouse)
Copy, converting formulas into values.	↵ ENTER

EXERCISES

9A **In this exercise, you enter data and formulas and copy them from one area of the worksheet to another.**

1. Enter the number 1000 in cell A2.
2. Copy the number in cell A2 to A5.
3. Copy the number in cell A5 to the range of cells B6..F6.
4. Copy the numbers in the range of cells B6..F6 to the range of cells C9..G9.
5. Erase the worksheet.
6. Enter the number 20000 in cell A2.
7. In cell B2, enter the formula +A2*1.1.
8. Copy the formula in cell B2 to cell C2.
9. Copy the formula in cell C2 to the range of cells D2..F2.
10. In cell A4, enter the formula +A2*.5.
11. In cell A5, enter the formula +A2+150.
12. Copy the formulas in cells A4 and A5 to the range of cells B4..F5.
13. Save the worksheet using the filename E09A.
14. Print the worksheet.

9B **In this exercise, you modify an existing worksheet to include additional information. You also copy information from various locations on the worksheet to other locations.**

1. Retrieve the E08B file.
2. Insert two rows at row 9.
3. Enter the text "Toasters" in cell A9 and "Stoves" in cell A10.
4. Copy the text in the range of cells A9..A10 to the range of cells A15..A16.
5. Center the text "Q3" in cell D6 and "Q4" in cell E6.
6. Center the text "Total" in cell F6.
7. Enter the number 1500 in cell B9 and the number 3000 in cell B10.
8. Enter the number 0.025 in cell C15 and the number 0.01 in cell C16.
9. Copy the numbers in the range of cells C13..C16 to the range of cells D13..E16.
10. Copy the formulas from cells C7..C8 to cells C9..C10.
11. Copy the formulas in the range of cells C7..C10 to the range of cells D7..E10.
12. Insert three rows at row 11.
13. Fill the range of cells B11..F11 with single underlining using the /Copy command.
14. Enter the text "Total" in cell A12.

15. Use the pointing method to create a formula in cell B12 to sum the product sales for all products during Q1.
16. Copy the formula in cell B12 to the range of cells C12..F12.
17. Use the pointing method to create a formula in cell F7 to determine total sales for the year for Washers.
18. Copy the formula in cell F7 to the range of cells F8..F10.
19. Fill the range of cells B13..F13 with double underlining.
20. Save the worksheet using the filename E09B.
21. Print the worksheet.

Changing the Appearance of a Worksheet

CONCEPTS

This topic addresses two issues related to the appearance of your worksheet: how to change column widths and how to change the way numerical values display.

> **TIP** The /Worksheet Column Column-Range command allows you to set and reset widths for a range of columns. The /Worksheet Column Reset-Width command removes the width assigned to a column and returns it to the global value.

> **TIP** To display the Global Settings sheet at any time, you can also use the /Worksheet Status command. Press the ENTER key to return to Ready mode.

Changing Column Widths

120

Adjusting the width of 1-2-3 columns is necessary for many reasons, and it is one of the most frequently performed activities. Columns that are too narrow can lead to truncated labels. Columns that are too wide limit the amount of information you can see on your screen or in your printed reports. Proper use of "white space" in your reports, as controlled by column width and blank lines, can improve readability.

In an empty worksheet, all columns use the **global column width**, which is nine characters. You change the value of the global column width with the /Worksheet Global Column-Width command. You can assign any column its own column width with the /Worksheet Column Set-Width command. A width assigned to a column takes precedence over the global width. Thus, any change you make to the global width does not affect columns that have been assigned their own width. ◄

The global column width is one of several **global settings** that affect the entire worksheet. When you select the /Worksheet Global command, 1-2-3 replaces the worksheet area with an information screen called the **Global Settings sheet**, which displays information about your computer configuration and the global settings that can be changed via the menu. Pressing the WINDOW (F6) key switches the screen between the Global Settings display and the view of the worksheet area. ◄

To change column widths either globally or individually, select the appropriate command sequence. 1-2-3 prompts you to enter the new value for the column width, displaying the old value as the suggested response. The mode indicator displays *POINT*. You can type a new value for the width or, often more conveniently, you can use the RIGHT or LEFT arrow key to increase or decrease the column width by 1 with each keystroke. 1-2-3 displays the effect in the worksheet area. When you have the correct width, press the ENTER key to make the change and return to Ready mode.

As you change the column width, the number of columns visible on the screen increases or decreases accordingly. Repeating labels adjust to fill the new column width and aligned labels maintain their proper position. Numerical values remain right aligned.

In practice, you usually set the global column width to the value that is appropriate for displaying most of your data. Then you change individual column widths where needed, for example, to handle long row labels or to provide extra width to display all of the digits in total columns. If the column has its own width, the expression [Wxx], where xx is the column width, appears in the current cell contents.

TIP Some formats require you to input the number of decimal places to display. These formats always display the specified number of decimal digits after the decimal point by rounding longer decimal values or adding trailing zeros, if necessary.

Changing the Way Values Are Displayed (121)

The way values display in the worksheet area is determined by their **format**. Initially the **global format** governs the display of all cells. However, you can assign each cell in the worksheet its own format, which overrides the global format.

You can change the global format with the /Worksheet Global Format command. The most commonly used format options are described in Table 10.1. The default format is the general format, which displays most numbers in a reasonable fashion. However, it does not use comma separators in large numbers, it does not always line up the decimal points in columns, and it may display more digits after the decimal point than are desirable. You can use other formats to overcome such limitations. ◀

Table 10.1
1-2-3 Formats

Format	Result
General	Default global format. Uses minus sign for negatives. Displays as many nonzero decimal digits as possible, truncating undisplayed digits. Switches to scientific notation to display values when number of digits to left of decimal point exceeds column width minus 1.
The following formats specify the number of decimal digits to be displayed, rounding the value to that many digits. The display of the value –1234.567 with 1 decimal place is shown.	
, (Comma)	Uses comma separator and parentheses for negative values. (1,234.6)
Currency	Uses dollar sign, comma separator, and parentheses for negative values. ($1,234.6)
Fixed	Uses minus sign for negative values. –1234.6
Percent	Multiplies values by 100 before displaying with trailing % symbol. -0.1234 displays as –12.3%

Sci	Displays numbers using scientific (exponential) notation. −1.2E+03
The following formats provide special capabilities.	
Date	Displays the integer part of a value as a date, using one of five different display formats. Integers are interpreted as the number of days since January 1, 1900.
Time	Displays the fractional part of a value as a time using one of four different display formats. Fractions are interpreted as the fraction of the day that has passed.
Hidden	Displays blank cell in worksheet area. Cell contents may be viewed in control panel.
Text	Displays the formula in a cell rather than its value. Truncates the formula display to the cell width.

TIP To reset the formats in all cells, run the /Range Format Reset command in cell A1 and then press END followed by HOME to highlight the entire active area.

You assign formats to individual cells with the /Range Format command. After selecting the format and, if requested, the number of decimal digits, you specify the range of cells to be formatted. 1-2-3 indicates that an individual format has been assigned to a cell by including the first character of the format and, if appropriate, the number of decimal digits between parentheses in the current cell contents. For example, (F1) would correspond to a fixed format with one decimal digit displayed and (,0) would indicate the comma format with no decimal digits or decimal point.

In addition to the formats shown in Table 10.1, 1-2-3 provides a /Range Format Reset command, which removes a format from a cell. The cells in the selected range revert to using the global format. ◀

You normally select the global format appropriate for most of your data values. For example, you might use a (,1) format if the majority of your values represent thousands of dollars with values running into the millions. You could then use a (C1) format in the first row or in total rows to put currency symbols on these key lines. Whole numbers such as number of personnel might be displayed with a (,0) format. You would need an (F0) format for years such as 1991. Ratios might be formatted using (,2) or (P1) to display sufficient digits or convert them to percentages.

TIP Another way to display values that are too large is to scale the values. Instead of displaying values in dollars you can choose thousands of dollars either by changing your input data or by using 1-2-3 formulas to divide the input figures by 1000.

If the column is too narrow to hold all the characters that the format of the value requires, 1-2-3 fills the cell display in the worksheet area with asterisks. This is in contrast to the way 1-2-3 handles labels that are too long to be displayed in the cell. 1-2-3 displays as much of the label as it can and truncates it when it reaches a nonempty cell. With values, however, 1-2-3 displays either the entire value or shows asterisks. To remove the asterisks and display the cell contents, you need to change the column width or the display format. ◀

Note that the /Range Erase command does *not* erase formats from cells. Furthermore, cells need not contain data in order to be formatted with the /Range Format command. You can use the /Range Format command to set up formats ahead of time so that numbers that are entered into the worksheet later will automatically display with the correct format. This is frequently done when you create templates (Topic 7). Using the /Copy or /Move command on cells containing formats copies and moves the formats as well as the data.

TUTORIAL

In this tutorial, you learn some techniques, such as adjusting column widths and changing formats, for creating an easy-to-read report. To begin this tutorial, you should have the REV09 worksheet on the screen.

1 Change column widths. The first step in improving the appearance of a worksheet is to modify the column widths so that they are appropriate for the length of the material. To begin, you change the width of the first column so that the entire label MISCELLANEOUS is visible.

Press	HOME	Moves to A1.

You can be anywhere in the column to change its width. The width of all the cells in the column are changed; you cannot change the width of just one cell.

Press	/, W, C, S	Selects Worksheet, Column, Set-Width.

> **TIP** You can also type in a fixed number of characters for the column width. The advantage to using the arrow keys is that you can immediately see how the new width looks.

The message "Enter column width (1..240): 9" is on the control panel.

Press	→ five times	Widens column A by five characters.

The value in the second line of the control panel is 14. You see [W14] in the current cell contents. The entire label MISCELLANEOUS is visible in A14.

Press	↵ ENTER	Locks in new width. ◀

Now make column D narrower.

Press	→ three times	Moves to column D.
Press	/, W, C, S	Selects Worksheet, Column, Set-Width.
Press	← twice	Narrows column D by two characters.
Press	↵ ENTER	Locks in new width.

The report heading in rows 1 and 2 is no longer well centered. Before modifying the number formats, you move the heading over.

Press	HOME	Moves to A1.
Press	/, M, ↓, ↵ ENTER	Selects Move with Move what? range the worksheet heading, A1..A2.
Press	→, ↵ ENTER	Moves heading to B1..B2.

Note that, when moving a column of cells, you must specify only the top cell(s) in the To where? range.

2 **Change the format of values.** You will now change the format for the values. This is done either through the /Worksheet command or the /Range command. Numerous options are available, and we encourage you to experiment on your own with a variety of formats. You first set the global format to Fixed, 1 decimal place.

Press	/, W, G	Selects Worksheet, Global.

When you select Global, a Global Settings sheet is displayed showing the current settings for the various global options.

Press	F, F	Selects Format, Fixed.

The message "Enter number of decimal places (0..15): 2" is on the control panel. You can set the number of decimal places to be displayed from 0 through 15 with 2 being the suggested number. Here you pick 1.

Type	1	
Press	↵ ENTER	Chooses 1 decimal place.

Negative numbers use a negative sign. Now you format various ranges. The choices for the formats are the same as at the worksheet level. First, you format the gross revenue values with a currency format.

Move to	B16	
Press	/, R, F, C	Selects Range, Format, Currency.

The message "Enter number of decimal places (0..15): 2" is on the control panel.

Press	↵ ENTER	Selects 2, the suggested number of decimal places.

The message "Enter range to format: B16..B16" is on the control panel. As usual, you select the range by pointing or by using the mouse.

Press	→ twice, ↵ ENTER	Chooses range B16..D16.

Note (C2) in the current cell contents for B16. This indicates that cell B16 has a format, currency with two decimal places. The asterisks in B16 through D16 indicate that, to be displayed in the (C2) format, the values in those cells require more characters than are available in the cell. To see the value, you must either change the column width or the cell format. You now change the format of the cells back to the global format using Reset.

Press	/, R, F, R	Selects Range, Format, Reset.

The message "Enter range to format: B16..B16" is on the control panel.

Press	→ twice, ↵ ENTER	Cancels range format for B16..D16.

The (C2) is gone from the current cell contents. You now set the format of the gross revenue values to currency with zero decimal places.

Press	/, R, F, C, 0	Selects Range, Format, Currency, 0.
Press	↵ ENTER, → twice, ↵ ENTER	Formats B16..D16 with (C0).

The current cell contents for B16 through D16 contain (C0). Note the $ and the commas in the cells in the worksheet area. Set the same format for the net revenue values.

Press	↓ three times	Moves to B19.
Press	/, R, F, C, 0	Selects Range, Format, Currency, 0.
Press	↵ ENTER, → twice, ↵ ENTER	Formats B19..D19 with (C0).

Format the percent of gross revenue row with a comma and one decimal place.

Press	↓	Moves to B20.
Press	/, R, F, ,, 1	Selects Range, Format, Comma, 1.
Press	↵ ENTER, → three times, ↵ ENTER	Formats B20..E20 with (,1).

Since many of the values in the worksheet are integers, you now reformat the worksheet with zero decimal places to enhance its appearance.

> **TIP** In general, cell options such as width and format override global settings.

Press	[/], [W], [G], [F]	Selects Worksheet, Global, Format.
Press	[,], [0], [↵ENTER]	Formats worksheet with (,0).

Note that the format of the cells set with a range format does not change and note that the negative numbers are in parentheses. Now format the revenue and change numbers for BOLTS with (C0). ◀

Move to	B7	
Press	[/], [R], [F], [C], [0]	Selects Range, Format, Currency, 0.
Press	[↵ENTER], [→] twice, [↵ENTER]	Formats B7..D7 with (C0).

You next format the percent change column with (,1).

Press	[→] three times	Moves to E7.
Press	[/], [R], [F], [,], [1]	Selects Range, Format, Comma, 1.
Press	[↵ENTER], [END], [↓], [↵ENTER]	Formats E7..E20 with (,1).

Note that there is no effect on the labels in cells E15 and E18. Formatting only affects values. You now change the column widths using a global command.

Press	[/], [W], [G], [C]	Selects Worksheet, Global, Column-Width.
Press	[←], [↵ENTER]	Narrows columns by one character.

There is no effect on the column widths set through the range option. Your worksheet should look like Figure 10.1. You now print, after adjusting the print range, and then save the worksheet.

Press	[/], [P], [P], [A], [R]	Selects Print, Printer, Align, Range.

The range is now B1..E25. Using the /Move command to move the worksheet heading from A1..A2 to B1..B2 has impacted the print range.

Press	[ESC]	Changes range address to cell address.

Figure 10.1
Formatted Revenue Worksheet

```
              ACE HARDWARE
         1991 REVENUE FORECAST

               PRIOR     PLAN              %
PRODUCT      REVENUE  REVENUE   CHANGE   CHANGE
-----------------------------------------------
BOLTS           $268     $300      $32     11.9
NAILS            200      225       25     12.5
NUTS             222      250       28     12.6
SCREWS           325      350       25      7.7
WASHERS          210      200     (10)    (4.8)
HINGES            10       30       20    200.0
BRACKETS          20       50       30    150.0
MISCELLANEOUS    12       18        6     50.0
               -----    -----    -----    -----
GROSS         $1,267   $1,423     $156     12.3
  ADJUST.        302      285     (17)    (5.8)
               -----    -----    -----    -----
NET             $965   $1,138     $173     18.0
  % GROSS       76.2     80.0      3.8      5.0

REV ADJ %                  20
===============================================
Figures prepared by R. E. Jones
11/17/91
```

Press	HOME, .	Moves to A1; anchors the cell pointer.
Move to	E25	
Press	↵ENTER	Selects new range A1..E25.
Press	G, P, Q	Selects Go, Page, Quit.
Press	/, F, S	Selects File, Save.
Type	REV10 ↵ENTER	Saves worksheet under REV10.

PROCEDURE SUMMARY

CHANGING COLUMN WIDTHS

To change the column width globally:

Cell pointer can be anywhere in worksheet.	(pointer-movement keys or mouse)
Activate the Main menu.	/
Select Worksheet.	W

Select Global.	G
Select Column-Width.	C
Choose the new column width.	(arrow keys or your input)
Lock in the selection.	↵ ENTER

To change the width of a single column:

Position cell pointer in column.	
Activate the Main menu.	/
Select Worksheet.	W
Select Column.	C
Select Set-Width.	S
Choose new width.	(arrow keys or your input)
Lock in the selection.	↵ ENTER

FORMATTING VALUES

To change the global format for cells containing values:

Activate the Main menu.	/
Select Worksheet.	W
Select Global.	G
Select Format.	F
Choose the format.	(your input)
If requested, enter the number of decimal places to be displayed.	(your input)
Enter the input and format the worksheet.	↵ ENTER

To change the format of a range of cells:

Move the cell pointer to the upper left corner of the range.	(pointer-movement keys or mouse)
Activate the Main menu.	/
Select Range.	R
Select Format.	F
Choose the format for the range.	(your input)
If requested, enter the number of decimal places to be displayed.	(your input)

Enter the input.	↵ENTER
Highlight the range to format.	(pointer-movement keys or mouse)
Format the range.	↵ENTER

EXERCISES

10A In this exercise, you retrieve, format, and save the template you created in Topic 7, and you enter data for Quarter 2.

1. Retrieve the QTRMAST file.
2. Change the width of column A to 13.
3. Change the width of column B to 7.
4. Assign a global format of (F0).
5. Assign a range format of (C0) to cell B9, gross revenue, and cell B12, net revenue.
6. Assign a range format of (F1) to cell B13, percent of gross.
7. Save the file using the name QTRMAST1.
8. Print the worksheet.
9. Enter the following values for the products: Nails - 61, Screws - 77, Bolts - 75, Nuts - 60, and Washers - 48.
10. Enter the value 51 for Adjustments.
11. Edit the heading of column B to "2nd QTR."
12. Edit the footnote to "Prepared by E. P. Michael on 7/14/91."
13. Save the file using the filename QTR2REV.
14. Print the worksheet.

10B In this exercise, you modify an existing worksheet and change the appearance of the data in the worksheet.

1. Retrieve the E09B file.
2. Edit the text in the range of cells A7..A10 so that two blank spaces appear at the beginning of each cell.
3. Edit the text in cell A12 so that four blank spaces appear at the beginning of the cell.
4. Change the width of column A to 10.
5. Set the global format to (,0).
6. Format the growth rates in the range of cells C16..E19 with a % sign and one decimal place.
7. Save the worksheet using the filename E10B.
8. Print the worksheet.

Protecting the Worksheet

CONCEPTS The 1-2-3 worksheet provides great flexibility in creating your applications. You can easily enter information anywhere you want in the worksheet, even in cells that are already occupied. However, once you have created your worksheet, this flexibility may become a drawback. If you accidentally hit the SPACEBAR while the cell pointer is in a cell containing a formula and then move from the cell, the formula is replaced. In the worksheet area, cells containing formulas look the same as cells containing numerical values. Thus a novice user assigned to do data entry may inadvertently enter new values over formulas. To address such problems, 1-2-3 provides commands that allow you to designate those cells in the worksheet that may be changed and to protect other areas from being modified.

Specifying Input Cells in a Worksheet 126

Most of the two million cells in a worksheet are not used for data entry. Usually the majority of them are empty. Many of the other cells should not be changed, especially those containing formulas or certain labels. The relatively few cells designed to accept input data are called the **input cells**.

1-2-3 worksheet cells may either be **protected** or **unprotected**. All cells are initially protected. 1-2-3 provides the /Range Unprot (for UNPROTect) command to allow you to unprotect input cells and distinguish them from the other cells in the worksheet. To unprotect a range of input cells, you place the cell pointer in a corner of the range, select the command, highlight the range of input cells, and press the ENTER key. ◀

> **TIP** Be sure to unprotect only cells that will contain input data. Do not unprotect cells that will remain blank.

In the worksheet area, 1-2-3 displays the contents of unprotected cells in color on color monitors or with greater intensity on monochrome monitors. When the cell pointer is in an unprotected cell, the current cell contents contain a capital "U." Note that empty unprotected cells look the same as empty protected cells when they do not contain the cell pointer. To make it clear where data is to be entered, it is sometimes desirable to enter zeros or a label such as "....." into the cells. This is easily accomplished using the /Copy command since this command will duplicate the protection status of the cell as well as the information. ◀

> **TIP** Remember that 1-2-3 interprets both empty cells and labels as zeros in formula computations.

If you inadvertently unprotect a cell that is not an input cell, you can use the /Range Prot (for PROTect) command to return it to its normal protected state. This command can also be used to change cells that initially were input cells back to their protected state. For example, in a worksheet that has input columns for each month, once the data for a month is entered, it should not be changed. The /Range Prot command is applied to the column after the data is entered.

Protecting a Worksheet from Change

126

Although worksheet cells are initially protected, you can still change their contents. To specify whether or not you can change protected cells, 1-2-3 uses the **global protection status**. Global protection may be either **enabled** or **disabled**. 1-2-3 displays the global protection status at the bottom of the Global Settings sheet that appears when you activate the /Worksheet Global command. In an empty worksheet, global protection is disabled and you can modify protected cells.

To activate global protection, you use the /Worksheet Global Protection Enable command. Once the protection is enabled, protected cells display the letters PR in the current cell contents. Then you may only enter data into the unprotected cells in the worksheet. If you attempt to enter information into a protected cell, 1-2-3 beeps and indicates *ERROR* in the mode indicator. The error message "Protected cell" appears in the center of your screen. The cell contents are not changed. To clear the error and return to Ready mode, press the ESCAPE key.

When global protection is enabled, commands such as /Copy and /Range Erase will work but only on unprotected cells. The /Worksheet Insert and Delete commands do not function. To make such changes to your worksheet, you use the /Worksheet Global Protection Disable command to disable global protection. Be sure to turn global protection back on after you are done. ◀

> **TIP** Note that the purpose of the 1-2-3 protection facilities is to help you avoid changing your worksheet by accident. It does not protect worksheets from intentional modifications since anyone familiar with the protection facilities can disable them.

TUTORIAL In this tutorial, you unprotect the input cells in the revenue worksheet. You then turn on the protection facility. This prevents crucial information, particularly formulas, from being accidentally overwritten. To begin this tutorial, you should have the REV10 worksheet on the screen.

1 Unprotect cells. You unprotect the cells containing the revenue values.

Move to	B7	
Press	/, R, U	Selects Range, Unprotect.

The message "Enter range to unprotect: B7..B7" is on line 2 of the control panel. Highlight through MISCELLANEOUS plan revenue, C14.

Move to	C14	Highlights B7..C14.
Press	↵ ENTER	Unprotects range B7..C14.

Note that the unprotected cells change color or intensity. Also note that the current cell contents of the unprotected cells contain a U. Now unprotect the adjustments that are input for the prior year, B17, and computed from a percent in the plan year, C22.

Move to	B17	
Press	/, R, U	Selects Range, Unprotect.
Press	↵ ENTER	Unprotects range B17..B17.
Move to	C22	
Press	/, R, U	Selects Range, Unprotect.
Press	↵ ENTER	Unprotects range C22..C22.

All cells containing input values are now unprotected.

2 **Turn on global protection.** You now turn on the protection facility.

Press	/, W, G	Selects Worksheet, Global.

The global settings are on the screen. Global protection is disabled.

Press	P, E	Selects Protection, Enable.

The current cell contents of protected cells contain a PR. On the Global Settings display, Global protection is Enabled. You now try to input some data to see how the protection works.

Move to	D7	
Type	50 ↵ ENTER	Mode indicator displays *ERROR*.

The contents of D7 are unchanged. The message "Protected cell" is in the middle of the screen. To return to Ready mode, press the Escape key.

Press	ESC	Returns to Ready mode.
Press	←	Moves to C7.
Type	210 ↵ ENTER	Enters 210 into C7.

The values displayed in the cells that depend on C7, such as D7 and C17, change. It is the underlying formulas in the cells that are protected and cannot be changed. Before you save the worksheet, you put the original value into C7. You also turn the protection off since you will be making more changes.

Type	300 ↵ ENTER	Enters 300 into C7.
Press	/, W, G, P, D	Selects Worksheet, Global, Protection, Disable.
Press	/, F, S	Selects File, Save.
Type	REV11 ↵ ENTER	Saves worksheet as REV11.

PROCEDURE SUMMARY

UNPROTECTING A RANGE OF CELLS

Move the cell pointer to the upper left corner of the range.	(pointer-movement keys or mouse)
Activate the Main menu.	/
Select Range.	R
Select Unprotect.	U
Highlight the range to unprotect.	(pointer-movement keys or mouse)
Unprotect the highlighted range.	↵ ENTER

PROTECTING CELLS

Activate the Main menu.	/
Select Worksheet.	W
Select Global.	G
Select Protection.	P
Turn the protection on or off.	E (on) or D (off)

EXERCISES

11A **In this exercise, you activate the protection feature in the template. Then you unprotect a range of cells.**

1. Retrieve the QTRMAST1 file.
2. Turn on the global protection.
3. Unprotect the range of cells B3..B7.
4. Unprotect cells B1, B10, and A16.
5. Save the worksheet using the filename QTRMAST2.

11B **In this exercise, you activate the protection feature in an existing worksheet. Then you unprotect a range of cells and change the data in some of the cells.**

1. Retrieve the E10B file.
2. Turn on the global protection.
3. Unprotect the range of cells C16..E19.
4. Change the number in cell D16 to 3.5% and the number in cell E16 to 2.5%.
5. Change the number in cell C18 to 2.8% and the number in cell E18 to 2.0%.
6. Change the number in cell E19 to 0.5%.
7. Save the worksheet using the filename E11B.
8. Print the worksheet.

Using Additional Computational Capabilities

CONCEPTS

This topic addresses several issues. We introduce the built-in computational functions you can use in 1-2-3. We discuss how some of these can be used effectively in the important case of summing columns. Finally, we discuss the construction of formulas and the use of the /Copy command when the formulas refer to specific cells.

Calculating with @ Functions

In addition to the basic arithmetic operations we have discussed so far, 1-2-3 provides additional computational capabilities through its **@ functions**, called "at" functions. Some of these functions perform standard financial calculations such as computing mortgage payments. Others perform mathematical calculations such as rounding and basic statistical analyses. Still others allow you to work with time and date information, manipulate character strings, make logical decisions, select information from tables, and display information about the 1-2-3 worksheet.

The use of all @ functions within a 1-2-3 expression follows a standard format. First comes the @ (at sign). This is followed by the function name indicating the calculation that the function performs such as SUM. Next, if information must be supplied to the @ function to perform its calculations, the information is enclosed within parentheses and follows immediately after the function name. If more than one piece of information is required, the different pieces are separated by commas within the parentheses. 1-2-3 refers to these pieces of information as **arguments**.

The arguments to an @ function may be references to cells or ranges in the worksheet, to constants, or to any 1-2-3 expression, even other @ functions. @AVG(B5..B25), which averages the values in the range B5 through B25, uses a single range as an argument. A complicated example is @ROUND(0.07*@SUM(B5..B25),2). The @ROUND function has two arguments enclosed in parentheses and separated by a comma. Its first argument is a 1-2-3 expression that multiplies the sum of the cells in the range B5 through B25 by 0.07. Its second argument, the number 2, indicates that the @ROUND function is to round the result of the first argument to two decimal places.

Summing Adjacent Cells

136

Probably the best known @ function is the @SUM (pronounced "at sum") function. This function calculates the sum of the numerical values contained in its arguments. The most common use of the @SUM function is to sum a single range of cells. For example, @SUM(B5..B25) sums the values in the cells from row 5 through row 25 in column B. However, the @SUM function sums any list of cells, ranges, constants, or expressions separated by commas. For example, the expression @SUM(B5..B25,-B30,0.1*B34) sums all the cells in the range B5 through B25, the negative of the value in cell B30, and 10 percent of the value in cell B34.

When cells or ranges are included in the arguments to @ functions, they can be entered in the expression by pointing or typing. Pointing to a cell or range is similar to the procedure we have used in 1-2-3 commands. When you reach the part of the expression requiring a range, you move the cell pointer to the first cell in the range, anchor the cell pointer using the period key, and then expand it to cover the entire range. The highlighted range is present in the entry. ◀

> **TIP** You enter the expression @SUM(B5..B15) by typing the initial @SUM(, moving the cell pointer to the cell B5, pressing the period key, and then expanding the highlight down to cell B15. Finally, you type the closing parenthesis.

Designing a Worksheet to Permit Changes

Using the @SUM function has a number of advantages over performing the summation with plus signs. Obviously, when many adjacent cells are involved, it is easier to specify a single range than to enumerate a long list of cells. These is also less chance for error.

However, using the @SUM function has another advantage. Frequently lists of data summed by the @SUM function are subject to change by either adding or deleting entries in the list. Just as with other ranges, as long as the insertion or deletion is done within the middle of the list, 1-2-3 automatically changes the summation range in the formula so that the formula remains correct. For example, the formula @SUM(B5..B15) sums the range of cells B5 through B15. Now insert two new rows between rows 11 and 12. Then cell B15 moves down to cell B17, and 1-2-3 adjusts the formula to read @SUM(B5..B17). Information entered into the new rows in column B is automatically included in the total.

Note, however, that new rows entered in row 5, at the beginning of the range, or in row 16, the next row below the range, are not included in the summation range. In the first case, the insertion moves both ends of the range so that it becomes B6 through B16, excluding the new cell. In the second case, neither of the cells is affected, so the range remains the same. ◀

> **TIP** Since insertions are frequently made at the top or bottom of a list, it is useful to include a cell of labels above and below the range to be summed and to include the cells in the summation range. Then insertions or deletions will always be made within the summation range. The total remains unchanged since the labels are treated as zeros.

Using Absolute References

To indicate which rows or columns in a formula need to remain fixed when the formula is copied, 1-2-3 uses the dollar sign $. Thus cell references written as $D2 or B$6 tell 1-2-3 that the column letter or row number following the $ refers to the actual column or row in the worksheet. They should not be changed when the formula is copied. 1-2-3 refers to a column or row reference preceded by a $ as an **absolute reference**. A cell reference containing an absolute reference to a row and a relative address to a column or vice versa is called a **mixed reference**. A cell reference in which both the row and column are preceded by $ is referred to as an **absolute cell reference**.

The ability to use absolute and relative cell references correctly when building formulas is crucial in order to avoid introducing errors into the worksheet when you copy the formulas. Figure 12.1(a) shows how the formula +A1+B2 in cell B3 changes when it is copied to three other cells, D3, D6, and B6. In relative terms, the formula in B3 refers to the cell two rows up and one column to the left (A1) plus the cell one row up in the same column (B2). In cell D6, for example, the cell two rows up and one column to the left is the cell C4. The cell one row up in the same column is the cell D5. Thus the result of copying the formula from B3 into D6 is +C4+D5.

Figure 12.1(a)

Copying with Relative References

	A	B	C	D	E
1					
2	Copy what? range B3				
3		+A1+B2		+C1+D2	To where? range D3
4					
5					
6		+A4+B5		+C4+D5	To where? range D6
7		To where? range B6			
8					

In Figure 12.1(b), the formula +$A1+B$2 in cell B3 uses mixed references. In copying the formula to the three other cells, D3, D6, and B6, the absolute references to column A and row 2 are unchanged, whereas the relative references to row 1 (that is, two rows up) and column B (that is, the same column) are modified appropriately. Again, in cell D6, for example, row 1 has changed to row 4 and column B has become column D.

Finally, in Figure 12.1(c), the formula +$A$1+$B$2 in cell B3 uses absolute cell references. Since these are not changed no matter where the formula is copied to, the formula is identical after being copied to the three cells, D3, D6, and B6.

Figure 12.1(b)
Copying with Mixed References

	A	B	C	D	E
1					
2	Copy what? range B3				
3		+$A1+B$2		+$A1+D$2	To where? range D3
4					
5					
6		+$A4+B$2		+$A4+D$2	To where? range D6
7		To where? range B6			
8					

Figure 12.1(c)
Copying with Absolute References

	A	B	C	D	E
1					
2	Copy what? range B3				
3		+$A$1+$B$2		+$A$1+$B$2	To where? range D3
4					
5					
6		+$A$1+$B$2		+$A$1+$B$2	To where? range D6
7		To where? range B6			
8					

To enter the $ symbols used for absolute references, you may use the F4 function key called the **ABSOLUTE key**. When you are building a formula by pointing and are pointing to a cell, pressing the absolute key cycles the cell reference through all possible combinations of absolute and relative references.

You can use the ABSOLUTE key to change references in Edit mode. Place the edit cursor in or to the right of the reference to be changed and press the ABSOLUTE key to cycle through the different possible combinations until you get the one you want. Alternatively you can enter the $ symbols directly in Edit mode by positioning the cursor where the symbol is to go and typing it.

Getting the absolute references right in a formula takes some practice. Most people learn by trial and error. If you are not quite sure what is needed, enter the formula with your best guess and then copy it into a few adjacent cells. Examine these cells to see if they are performing the calculation you want. If there is an error, you should be able to easily recognize what has changed that shouldn't or what didn't change that should have. Then go back, reenter the formula or edit the references, and try again until you get it correct and can complete the copy. After a while, you will recognize the types of formulas you use in your applications and will get the references correct the first time.

TUTORIAL By now you should have noticed that the total formulas at the bottom of the columns of revenue values do not behave well when the worksheet is modified. Any time a product is inserted or deleted, the formula must be edited manually. In this tutorial, you learn how to handle this issue using the @SUM function. To begin this tutorial, you should have the REV11 worksheet on the screen.

1 Create an @SUM formula. In this section you add the revenue values using the @SUM formula. You could first erase the current formulas (perhaps a good exercise in erasing ranges), but this is not necessary as 1-2-3 simply replaces the old formula with the new one.

You now create an @SUM formula in B16. As always, you select the range to sum by pointing.

Move to	B16	
Type	@SUM(	Begins to enter @SUM function.

You move the cell pointer to the prior revenue for BOLTS, B7.

Move to	B7	Enters B7 in formula.

The formula is @SUM(B7. The mode indicator displays *POINT*.

Press	[.]	Anchors cell pointer.
Press	[↓] seven times	Highlights prior revenue values, B7..B14.
Type	)	Closes parentheses.
Press	[↵ ENTER]	B16 displays $1,267.

The formula @SUM(B7..B14) has been entered in B16. You now copy the formula to plan revenue and change columns, C16 and D16.

Press	[/], [C], [↵ ENTER]	Selects Copy with Copy what? range B16..B16.
Press	[→], [.], [→], [↵ ENTER]	Copies formula to C16..D16.
Press	[→]	Moves to C16.

Examine the adjusted formula in the current cell contents.

2 **Handle insertion easily.** In this section you see how easily @SUM handles modifications to the product list especially if the original formula is well designed. First you insert a new row 14 for a new product.

Move to	A14	
Press	/, W, I, R, ↵ENTER	Selects Worksheet, Insert, Row; inserts a new row 14.
Type	TACKS →	Enters TACKS; moves to B14.
Type	15, ↓ three times	Enters 15 in B14; moves to B17.

Cell B17 displays 1282. The current cell contents are now @SUM(B7..B15). The inserted row has automatically been included in the range being added.

Press	↑ three times, →	Moves to C14.
Type	20 →, ↑	Enters 20 in C14; C17 displays 1443; moves to D13.

You now copy the change and percent change formulas from BRACKETS, D13..E13 to TACKS, D14..E14.

Press	/, C, →, ↵ENTER	Selects Copy with Copy what? range D13..E13.
Press	↓, ↵ENTER	Copies formulas from D13..E13 to D14..E14.

Note that when copying a row, you have to specify only the left end of the To where? range. The formula in D17 has been recalculated. Now delete the new product.

Press	↓	Moves to row 14.
Press	/, W, D, R, ↵ENTER	Selects Worksheet, Delete, Row; deletes row 14.

The sum formulas in what is now row 16 again have been readjusted with the deleted row removed from the formula. Now add a new row after the MISCELLANEOUS row.

Press	↓	Moves to row 15.
Press	/, W, I, R, ↵ENTER	Selects Worksheet, Insert, Row; inserts a new row 15.
Press	END, ←	Moves to A15.

Type	TACKS [→]	Enters TACKS; moves to B15.
Type	15 [→]	Enters 15; moves to C15.

The value displayed and the formula in B17 do not change. Rows (and columns) inserted at the edge of a range are not automatically included in the range. You will see the same situation when new values are included in columns C and D.

Type	20 [→], [↑]	Enters 20; moves to D14.
Press	[/], [C], [→], [↵ ENTER]	Selects Copy with Copy what? range D14..E14.
Press	[↓], [↵ ENTER]	Copies formulas from D14..E14 to D15..E15.

3 **Build an optimal @SUM formula.** To handle the problem of inserting rows at the top or bottom of the range, you include the cells containing the underlining as part of the formula. They are labels and so are assigned the value 0 in the formula. You build the formula in prior revenue and then copy to plan revenue and change.

Move to	B17	
Type	@SUM(	Begins @SUM formula.
Move to	B6	Moves to underlining at top of column.
Press	[.], [↓] ten times	Highlights data plus two underlinings, B6..B16.
Type	)	Closes parentheses.
Press	[↵ ENTER]	B17 displays 1282.
Press	[/], [C], [↵ ENTER]	Selects Copy with Copy what? range B17..B17.
Press	[→], [.], [→], [↵ ENTER]	Copies B17 to C17..D17.

You now can insert a new product anywhere between the underlinings and the totals adjust correctly. You enter a product and the prior and plan revenue data in a new row 16. Then copy the change and percent change formulas to the new row.

Press	[↑], [←]	Moves to A16.
Press	[/], [W], [I], [R], [↵ ENTER]	Selects Worksheet, Insert, Row; inserts a new row 16.

Type	DOOR KNOBS (→)	Enters DOOR KNOBS; moves to B16.
Type	60, (↓) twice	Enters 60; moves to B18.

Note that the value and the @SUM formula are correct.

Press	(↑) twice, (→)	Moves to C16.
Type	75 (→), (↑)	Enters 75; moves to D15.
Press	(/), (C), (→), (↵ ENTER), (↓), (↵ ENTER)	Copies formulas from D15..E15 to D16..E16.

Note that the formats from cells D15 and E15 are copied to D16 and E16. Now delete rows 15 and 16. The formulas readjust correctly.

Press	(/), (W), (D), (R), (↓), (↵ ENTER)	Select Worksheet, Delete, Row; deletes rows 15 and 16.

4 **Use absolute reference.** In column F, you input formulas to convert the plan revenue of each product to percent of total revenue. Since the denominator in the formula is always C16, the cell address C16 must be entered into the formula as an absolute reference so that it will copy correctly. First you enter column headings.

Move to	F4	
Type	^% (↓)	Enters % centered; moves to F5.
Type	"REV. (↓)	Enters REV.; moves to F6.
Type	\- (↓)	Fills F6 with underlining; moves to F7.
Build	100*C7/C16	

TIP Actually you only need to make the row reference absolute since you always want row 16. Here the column reference will behave correctly either way.

You need to make the cell reference C16 absolute so it will not change when copied. ◀

Press	(F2), (F4), (↵ ENTER)	Enters Edit mode; converts C16 to $C$16.
Press	(/), (C), (↵ ENTER)	Selects Copy with Copy what? range F7..F7.
Press	(↓), (.), (↓) six times, (↵ ENTER)	Copies formula from BOLTS, F7 to the other products, F8..F14.
Press	(↓) four times	Moves to F11.

In cell F11, the formula has become 100*C11/$C$16. The relative reference in the numerator has changed, but the absolute reference in the denominator has not. Your worksheet should look like Figure 12.2.

Figure 12.2
Completed Revenue Worksheet

ACE HARDWARE
1991 REVENUE FORECAST

PRODUCT	PRIOR REVENUE	PLAN REVENUE	CHANGE	% CHANGE	% REV.
BOLTS	$268	$300	$32	11.9	21
NAILS	200	225	25	12.5	16
NUTS	222	250	28	12.6	18
SCREWS	325	350	25	7.7	25
WASHERS	210	200	(10)	(4.8)	14
HINGES	10	30	20	200.0	2
BRACKETS	20	50	30	150.0	4
MISCELLANEOUS	12	18	6	50.0	1
	-----	-----	-----	-----	
GROSS	$1,267	$1,423	$156	12.3	
ADJUST.	302	285	(17)	(5.8)	
	-----	-----	-----	-----	
NET	$965	$1,138	$173	18.0	
% GROSS	76.2	80.0	3.8	5.0	
REV ADJ %		20			

Figures prepared by R. E. Jones
11/17/91

Finally, print and save the worksheet.

Press	/, P, P, A	Selects Print, Printer, Align.
Press	R, →, ↵ ENTER	Selects Range; includes column F in print range.
Press	G, P, Q	Selects Go, Page, Quit.
Press	/, F, S	Selects File, Save.
Type	REV12 ↵ ENTER	Saves worksheet under REV12.

PROCEDURE SUMMARY

SUMMING ADJACENT CELLS

Move the cell pointer to the cell in which you want to enter the formula.	(pointer-movement keys or mouse)
Begin the formula by typing the function and the open parenthesis.	@SUM(
Move the cell pointer to the upper left corner of the range.	(pointer-movement keys or mouse)
Anchor the cell pointer.	.
Highlight the range.	(pointer-movement keys or mouse)
Complete the formula by typing the close parenthesis.	)
Enter the formula.	↵ ENTER

EXERCISES

12A In this exercise, you modify the template and then enter data for Quarter 3.

1. Retrieve the QTRMAST2 file and turn off the global protection.
2. Enter the formula @SUM(B2..B8) in cell B9 by pointing.
3. Insert a new row 1.
4. Enter the label "%" centered in cell C1.
5. Enter the label "Gross" right aligned in cell C2.
6. Change the width of column C to 7.
7. Enter underlinings in cell C3.
8. Enter a formula for percent of Gross (100 times revenue for Nails divided by Gross Revenue) in cell C4.
9. Copy the formula to cells C5..C8.
10. Save the worksheet using the filename QTRMAST3.
11. Enter the following values for the products: Nails - 61, Screws - 79, Bolts - 73, Nuts - 64, and Washers - 55.

Be sure the formulas for percent of gross are correct. If not, edit them in QTRMAST2 and save again.

12. Enter the value 61 for adjustments.
13. Change the column heading in cell B2 to "3rd QTR."

14. Edit the footnote to "Prepared by E. P. Michael on 8/15/91."
15. Print the worksheet.
16. Save the worksheet using the filename QTR3REV.

12B In this exercise, you modify an existing worksheet to include the @SUM function.

1. Retrieve the E11B file.
2. Turn off the global protection.
3. Edit the formula in cell B12 so that it appears as @SUM(B6..B11).
4. Copy the formula in cell B12 to the range of cells C12..F12.
5. Insert a column at column B.
6. Insert a column at column G.
7. Fill cell G11 with single underlining.
8. Fill cell G13 with double underlining.
9. Change the column width of columns B and G to 1.
10. Edit the formula in cell H7 so that it appears as @SUM(B7..G7).
11. Copy the formula from cell H7 to cells H8 through H10.
12. Save the worksheet using the filename E12B.
13. Print the worksheet.

12C Create the worksheet on page 138, which you will use in the following tutorials.

1. Enter the headings in rows 1 through 3, centering appropriately.
2. Enter the column headings "PRODUCT" through "TOTAL" in the range A5..O5 with the ones in C through O right aligned.
3. Enter the underlinings in cell C6 and copy under the remaining headings.
4. Enter the product names in the range of cells A7..A12. Make three more copies using the /Copy command.
5. Fill in the REGION column making appropriate use of the /Copy command.
6. Enter the data values.
7. Enter a formula in cell O7 to total the data in row 7. Use @SUM and pointing.
8. Copy the formula to the other rows.
9. Set the global format to (F1).
10. Set the width of column A to 15, that of column B to 9, and the global width to 7.
11. Save the worksheet using the name REVMTH.

ACE HARDWARE
1991 DETAILED REVENUE FORECAST
(in thousands)

PRODUCT	REGION	JAN	FEB	MARCH	APRIL	MAY	JUNE	JULY	AUG	SEPT	OCT	NOV	DEC	TOTAL
BOLTS	NORTH	4.8	6.4	5.6	8.8	8.0	10.4	4.0	4.8	7.2	4.8	6.4	8.8	80.0
NAILS	NORTH	3.0	4.0	3.5	5.5	5.0	6.5	2.5	3.0	4.5	3.0	4.0	5.5	50.0
NUTS	NORTH	3.6	4.8	4.2	6.6	6.0	7.8	3.0	3.6	5.4	3.6	4.8	6.6	60.0
SCREWS	NORTH	6.0	8.0	7.0	2.4	10.0	1.0	5.0	6.0	9.0	6.0	8.0	11.0	79.4
WASHERS	NORTH	2.4	3.2	2.8	1.2	4.0	2.0	2.0	2.4	3.6	2.4	3.2	4.4	33.6
MISCELLANEOUS	NORTH	1.2	1.6	1.4	2.4	2.0	1.3	1.0	1.2	1.8	1.2	1.6	2.2	18.9
BOLTS	WEST	2.4	3.2	2.8	1.2	4.0	1.5	2.0	2.4	3.6	2.4	3.2	4.4	33.1
NAILS	WEST	1.2	2.0	1.8	1.8	2.5	2.5	1.3	1.5	2.3	1.5	2.0	2.8	23.2
NUTS	WEST	1.8	2.4	2.1	3.0	3.0	1.0	1.5	1.8	2.7	1.8	2.4	3.3	26.8
SCREWS	WEST	3.0	4.0	3.5	1.2	5.0	0.5	2.5	3.0	4.5	3.0	4.0	5.5	39.7
WASHERS	WEST	1.2	1.6	1.4	0.6	2.0	2.6	1.0	1.2	1.8	1.2	1.6	2.2	18.4
MISCELLANEOUS	WEST	0.6	0.8	0.7	3.6	1.0	1.3	0.5	0.6	0.9	0.6	0.8	1.1	12.5
BOLTS	SOUTH	3.6	4.8	4.2	2.1	6.0	7.8	3.0	3.6	5.4	3.6	4.8	6.6	55.5
NAILS	SOUTH	2.1	3.0	2.6	2.4	3.8	4.9	1.9	2.3	3.4	2.3	3.0	4.1	35.8
NUTS	SOUTH	2.4	3.6	3.2	4.2	4.5	5.9	2.3	2.7	4.1	2.7	3.6	5.0	44.2
SCREWS	SOUTH	4.2	6.0	5.3	1.8	7.5	9.8	3.8	4.5	6.8	4.5	6.0	8.3	68.5
WASHERS	SOUTH	1.8	2.4	2.1	0.6	3.0	3.9	1.5	1.8	2.7	1.8	2.4	3.3	27.3
MISCELLANEOUS	SOUTH	0.6	1.2	1.1	1.6	1.5	2.0	0.8	0.9	1.4	0.9	1.2	1.7	14.9
BOLTS	CENTRAL	1.2	1.6	1.4	0.8	2.0	2.6	1.0	1.2	1.8	1.2	1.6	2.2	18.6
NAILS	CENTRAL	0.6	1.0	0.9	1.4	1.3	1.6	0.6	0.8	1.1	0.8	1.0	1.4	12.5
NUTS	CENTRAL	0.6	1.2	1.1	1.7	1.5	2.0	0.8	0.9	1.4	0.9	1.2	1.7	15.0
SCREWS	CENTRAL	1.2	2.0	1.8	2.8	2.5	3.3	1.3	1.5	2.3	1.5	2.0	2.8	25.0
WASHERS	CENTRAL	0.6	0.8	0.7	1.1	1.0	1.3	0.5	0.6	0.9	0.6	0.8	1.1	10.0
MISCELLANEOUS	CENTRAL	0.0	0.4	0.4	0.6	0.5	0.7	0.3	0.3	0.5	0.3	0.4	0.6	5.0

Checkpoint 2

What You Should Know

- ✓ The contents of a cell can be edited by using the F2 key.
- ✓ Rows and columns can be inserted and deleted at any time.
- ✓ The contents of a cell can be copied or moved from one location on a worksheet to another location.
- ✓ Formulas can be copied or moved from one or more cells to other cells.
- ✓ The format of any number in a worksheet can be changed.
- ✓ The contents of a cell can be protected so that they cannot be changed.
- ✓ Lotus 1-2-3 contains many special functions that simplify computational procedures.

Review Questions

1. How can you change existing text or numbers in a worksheet?
2. What is the process for moving information from one location to another on a worksheet?
3. What is the process for copying information from one location to another on a worksheet?
4. How do you protect cells from being changed on a worksheet?
5. What are the methods for inserting and deleting rows and columns?
6. What special function is used to add numbers in a contiguous range of cells?
7. How do you change the column width of several columns at the same time?

CHECKPOINT PROBLEM A

In this problem, you modify and expand an existing worksheet.

1. Retrieve the CP1PA file.
2. Erase the ranges of cells B12..E12 and E5..E10.
3. Insert a row at row 5.
4. Enter the text "Sunday" in cell A5.
5. Insert a column at column D.
6. Right align the text "Goggles" in cell D3.
7. Enter the numbers 20, 38, 40, and 52 in cells B5 through E5.

8. Enter the numbers 45, 76, 85, 65, 70, and 95 in cells D6 through D11.
9. Copy cell C12 to cell D12.
10. Fill cell B4 with underlining. Copy cell B4 to the range of cells C4..F4.
11. In cell B13, enter a formula that uses the @SUM function to sum the range of cells B4..B12. Copy cell B13 to the range of cells C13..F13.
12. Insert a column at column B.
13. Insert a column at column G.
14. Copy cell F12 to cell G12 and cell F4 to cell G4.
15. Change the column width for columns B and G to 1.
16. In cell H5, enter a formula that uses the @SUM function to sum the range of cells B5..G5.
17. Copy the formula in cell H5 to the range of cells H6..H11.
18. Format the worksheet to insert commas and have zero decimal places.
19. In cell H15, calculate the average daily sales quantity. Use one decimal place for formatting purposes.
20. Enter text "Average Daily Sales" in cell A15.
21. Move cell C1 to cell D1.
22. Save the worksheet using the filename CP2PA.
23. Print the worksheet.

CHECKPOINT PROBLEM B

In this problem, you modify and expand an existing worksheet.

1. Retrieve the CP1PB file.
2. Change the text in cell A8 so "Gross Profit" appears in the cell.
3. Change the text in cell A11 so "Net Income" appears in the cell.
4. Widen column A so that the entire label "Gross Profit" is displayed in the column in the worksheet area.
5. Format all cells in the worksheet with (,0).
6. Place a $ before each number in the Sales and Net Income rows.
7. Format the range of cells B18..D19 so that two decimal places appear.
8. Activate the global protection.
9. Unprotect the ranges of cells B18..D19 and cells B5..D5 in the worksheet.
10. Enter the numbers 0.59, 0.58, and 0.55 in cells B18 through D18.
11. Enter the number 0.35 in cells B19 through D19.
12. Format cell E14 to include a $.
13. Save the worksheet using the filename CP2PB.
14. Print the worksheet.

Working with Large Worksheets

CONCEPTS Of necessity, most of the worksheets presented in a book such as this are small. We want you to be able to see the application on your screen so that you can understand it clearly. In reality, programs such as 1-2-3 are often used for large applications where you can only see a fraction of the application on your screen at one time. Your interaction with 1-2-3 changes significantly when you work with these large applications. Part of the difference is psychological because you must work from a mental, rather than a visual, picture of the worksheet.

Pointing methods become very important. If you cannot see the cells to be included in a formula, you probably will not (and should not) remember their addresses. Therefore you cannot type them into the formulas without first locating them. When you locate cells by pointing, 1-2-3 automatically enters the cell addresses into the formulas for you.

With large worksheets, changes become more problematic. You must be sure that when you insert or delete rows or move blocks that the action will not damage portions of the worksheet that are not on the screen. You also must be sure that when you modify one part of the worksheet, other areas requiring related modifications are properly adjusted. In this topic we examine some facilities 1-2-3 provides for handling large worksheets.

Viewing with Titles

150

Many 1-2-3 applications have an initial column of labels that describe the contents of each row. Similarly, near the top of the worksheet will be one or more rows of labels that contain column headings. When you view the lower rows or the rightmost columns in a large worksheet, the descriptive labels are no longer on the screen, which makes it difficult to know the meaning of the values in the worksheet area.

To alleviate this problem, 1-2-3 allows you to keep certain rows and columns visible at the edges of the worksheet area. 1-2-3 calls these rows and columns **titles**, corresponding to their most common use, which is to provide descriptive titles for the information being viewed.

Titles are established using the /Worksheet Titles command. This command allows you to create titles horizontally, vertically, or in both directions. Having determined which rows and columns you want to have remain on the screen, you position the screen so that the first column in the vertical title is at the left edge of the worksheet area and the top row in the horizontal title is at the top of the worksheet area. You then place the cell pointer immediately to the right of the last column and directly below the last row in the titles. Finally, you execute the command. To remove titles from the worksheet, you use the /Worksheet Titles Clear command. ◄

> **TIP** To position the worksheet area, you can press the SCROLL LOCK key to turn on scrolling. This allows you to use the arrow keys to move the screen directly. Be sure to turn scrolling off again after you have positioned the worksheet.

When 1-2-3 is in Ready mode, you cannot penetrate the titles area with the standard movement keys. Thus, if you have set column A and rows 4 and 5 to be titles, pressing the HOME key moves the cell pointer to cell B6 rather than A1. You can move into the title area when 1-2-3 is in Point mode. In particular, you use the GOTO (F5) function key to move to cells. When you move into the title area, the title rows and/or columns are still present at the edges of the worksheet area. You will see an initial doubling of the titles, which may be confusing. Just remember that the area to the right and/or below the titles is used to view the entire worksheet as though the titles were not there. To remove the doubling, page down or right as many times as needed.

Using Windows to Work in Two Parts of a Worksheet (150)

> **TIP** After you have created the windows, you can change the areas of the worksheet that they view. Therefore the important issue when you position your cell pointer is how large each window will be, not what rows or columns are in them initially.

> **TIP** If you want to make permanent changes in these settings when two windows are present, be sure the changes are made in the upper or left window.

> **TIP** Once you unsynchronize windows, future windows will be unsynchronized even though you use the /Worksheet Window Clear command. To synchronize the windows again, you use the /Worksheet Window Sync command.

Titles allow you to view different nonadjacent portions of the worksheet simultaneously. 1-2-3 also allows you to split the worksheet area into two windows that allow you to both view and *work in* separate areas.

Windows are created using the /Worksheet Window command. This command allows you to establish one pair of either vertical or horizontal windows. The position of the cell pointer determines where the worksheet area splits and hence the size of each window.

When you create horizontal windows, 1-2-3 inserts a new horizontal border containing column letters at the position of the cell pointer. The row you were in slides down to become the top row of the bottom window. The cell pointer is in the previous row, which is now the last row visible in the top window. Vertical windows act similarly with columns instead of rows. ◀

Each window created acts the same as the initial single window but in miniature. Within either window you may move the cell pointer to any part of the worksheet, enter data, and create formulas. To move the cell pointer between the two windows, you use the WINDOW (F6) key.

Initially the two windows have the same global settings and column widths. Once they are created, however, you can set different individual and global column widths, global formats, and titles in the two windows. Changes made to individual cells appear in both windows. To return to a single window, you use the /Worksheet Window Clear command. The settings of the resulting single window as well as the area being viewed come from the upper or left window. ◀

1-2-3 also allows you to control the relationship between the rows seen in vertical windows. By default, the two windows are **synchronized**, which means that both vertical windows display the same rows. You can use synchronized windows to view a total column at the far right of a wide worksheet in the right window while you examine the details of the worksheet in the left window. As you page down in the left window, the rows present in the right window change in tandem, keeping the proper totals visible. With unsynchronized windows, the columns or rows visible in one window need have no relationship to those visible in the other window. Unsynchronized windows are particularly useful when you need to work in two different areas of the worksheet. ◀

You can use the WINDOW (F6) key while pointing in 1-2-3 commands and formulas. Suppose you are in one part of the worksheet building formulas that rely on data in a distant part of the worksheet. You create two windows in the worksheet area. You position the cells in which you are building your formulas and the cell pointer in one window and the area from which you are getting your data in the second window. You start the command or function. Then, to specify a cell or range, you press the WINDOW (F6) key to shift into the second window and point to the cells. When you type a symbol or press ENTER, 1-2-3 moves the cell pointer into the first window to the current cell.

> **TIP** The /Worksheet Column Hide command can be used to hide some of the columns in a large worksheet so that columns that would normally be separated are temporarily adjacent.

Other Large Worksheet Techniques

Worksheets can be organized in various ways that enhance the usefulness of the 1-2-3 commands. For example, total rows and columns are traditionally placed at the extreme right or the bottom of worksheets. To take better advantage of titles, which freeze information on the top and left, you might place your totals, or even a second set of totals, at the top or the left in your worksheets where they can then be included in the titles area. ◀

Another technique is to create summary areas containing key information from different parts of the worksheet. You can transfer the data in one cell to another cell using a simple formula that consists of a plus sign and the address of the source cell. For example, if cell C75 contains the total sales figure, the formula +C75 in cell AA6 displays the total sales in cell AA6. By creating several such formulas that display key information and viewing them through a window, you can make changes to your input data and simultaneously see the impact on very different results.

Finally you should consider organizing your worksheet using a **block diagonal** structure. In this organization, each of the different blocks that make up your worksheet is created to the right of and below other blocks so that they have no rows or columns in common. Therefore rows and columns can be inserted and deleted and column widths changed in one block without affecting any other block.

TUTORIAL

In this tutorial, you learn titles and windows, useful for working in large worksheets. To start the tutorial, you should have the large worksheet REVMTH created in the last exercises on the screen. It should have a global format of 1 fixed decimal place, a global column width of 7, column A with a width of 15, and column B with a width of 9.

1 **Set titles.** In this section, you solve the problem of keeping the row and column headings on the screen. You use the rows with the months and underlinings and the columns with the products and regions as titles. Thus A5 is the top row and first column of the titles. You position cell A5 in the upper left corner of the screen. Then you put the cell pointer in cell C7, which is the cell to the right of and below the titles.

Press	HOME	
Press	SCROLL LOCK	Turns on SCROLL indicator.

With the SCROLL LOCK feature on, the screen moves down, across the worksheet, with the cell pointer staying at the top of the screen.

Press	↓ four times	

A5 is in the upper left corner of the screen.

Press	SCROLL LOCK	Turns off SCROLL indicator.
Press	↓ twice, → twice	Moves to C7.
Press	/, W	Selects Worksheet.
Press	T, B	Selects Titles, Both.

Selecting Both sets both horizontal and vertical titles. You have frozen rows 5 and 6 and columns A and B on the screen. The effect of setting titles becomes apparent only when you move around the worksheet.

Press	END, ↓	Moves to C30.

Rows 5 and 6 are still on the screen.

Press	END, →	Moves to O30.

Columns A and B are still on the screen.

Press	HOME	Moves to C7, not A1.
Press	↑	No movement; program beeps.

You cannot move the cell pointer into the title area with the movement keys when in Ready mode.

2 **Work with titles set.** You continue to develop the worksheet by entering column and row totals. You start with a label for the column total row in A32. The GoTo (F5) key moves the cell pointer into the titles.

Press	F5	
Type	A32 ↵ENTER	Moves to A32.

Note that columns A and B appear twice on the screen. The titles are still frozen on the screen.

Type	"MONTHLY TOTAL	
Press	(→) twice, (↑)	Enters MONTHLY TOTAL right aligned in A32; moves to C31.

Since cell A32 appears on the screen twice, the phrase MONTHLY TOTAL appears twice. But there is only one cell A32. Now enter double underlining and a formula for column totals at the bottom of the January column, C. The formula includes the underlinings at the top, C6, and the bottom, C31, of the column.

Type	"= = = = = (↓)	Underlines values in column C.
Type	@SUM(	
Press	(↑), (END), (↑), (↓)	Moves to C6.

Because you are in Point mode, you enter the column title area. Note the use of the End key to move to the top of the column, C5. The End key is extremely useful for moving in large worksheets.

Press	(.), (END), (↓)	Highlights C6..C31.
Type	) (↑)	Enters @SUM(C6..C31) in C32; moves to C31.

Copy the underlinings, C31, and sum formula, C32, to under the rest of the monthly and total columns, D through O. Pay close attention to the highlighting of the To where? range.

Press	(/), (C), (↓), (↵ ENTER)	Selects Copy with Copy what? range C31..C32.
Press	(→), (.), (↑), (END), (→), (↓) twice, (↵ ENTER)	Copies contents of C31..C32 to D31..O32.

To copy column C31..C32 to many columns, you only have to specify the first row of the columns as the To where? range.

3 **Set windows.** In this section, you set windows and use them to view data.

Press	(→)	Moves to D31.
Press	(/), (W)	Selects Worksheet.
Press	(W), (V)	Selects Window, Vertical.

The screen is divided into two windows with the cell pointer in the left window. A copy of the column of row numbers is inserted between columns C and D. You now move the cell pointer to the other window using the Window (F6) key.

Press	(F6)	Shifts to right window.

The cell pointer is in cell D31 in the right window. Two columns are visible in the right window.

Press	END, →	Moves to O31.

The column with the row totals is visible in the right window.

Press	F6	Shifts back to left window.
Press	/, W, W, S	Selects Worksheet, Window, Synchronize.
Press	PAGE UP	

Both windows move up eighteen rows. You can view the row totals in the right window as you view and enter data in the left window.

Press	/, W, W, U	Selects Worksheet, Window, Unsynchronize.
Press	PAGE DOWN	

Only the left window moves down eighteen rows. In Unsynchronize mode, only the window the cell pointer is in moves. You now return to Synchronize mode for future use, clear the windows, and remove the double image of columns A and B.

Press	/, W, W, S	Selects Worksheet, Window, Synchronize.
Press	/, W, W, C	Selects Worksheet, Window, Clear.
Press	CTRL-→	Moves to F31.

The columns appear once. You save the worksheet to use in Topic 14.

Press	HOME	Moves to C7.
Press	/, F, S	Selects File, Save.
Type	REVMH131 ↵ENTER	Saves worksheet under REVMH131.

4 **Insert subtotals.** You now insert subtotals for each region in the monthly columns. You start by inserting new rows and underlining.

Move to	C13	
Press	/, W, I, R	Selects Worksheet, Insert, Row.
Press	↓ twice, ↵ENTER	Inserts three new rows.
Type	\- ↓	Fills C13 with underlining.

Now enter a label and subtotal formula in row 14. You must use the GoTo (F5) key to move to A14 in the titles.

Press	F5	
Type	A14 ↵ENTER	Moves to A14.
Type	^Subtotal	
Press	→ twice	Enters Subtotal centered in A14; moves to C14.
Type	@SUM(	
Press	↑, END, ↑, ↓, .	Points to and anchors in underlining for Jan, C6.
Press	END, ↓,), ↑	Enters formula; moves to C13.

The formula totals from underlining to underlining, C6..C13. You now copy the underlining and the subtotal formulas from the Jan column to the columns for the other months and the row total.

Press	/, C, ↓, ↵ENTER	Selects Copy with Copy what? range C13..C14.
Press	→, ., ↑, END, →	Anchors To where? range in D13; highlights D13..O12.
Press	↓ twice, ↵ENTER	Copies to D13..O14.

Now you insert three new rows and copy the underlinings, label, and formulas from the NORTH region to the WEST region.

Press	F5	
Type	A22 ↵ENTER	Moves to A22.
Press	/, W, I, R	Selects Worksheet, Insert, Row.
Press	↓ twice, ↵ENTER	Inserts three new rows.

Now you copy starting in the To where? range.

Press	/, C, ESC, ↑ nine times	Selects Copy; moves to blank cell above Subtotal in NORTH, A13.
Press	., → twice, END, →	
Press	↓, ↵ENTER	Selects A13..O14 as Copy what? range; returns to A22.
Press	↵ENTER	Selects A22 as To where? range.

TIP To move between windows using a mouse, move the mouse pointer to a cell in the desired window and click the mouse button.

The subtotal data for NORTH is copied to WEST. As an exercise, repeat the preceding steps, inserting and copying, starting first in A31 for the SOUTH region and then in A40 for the CENTRAL. You are in A40 at the bottom of the worksheet area.

5 **Work with windows.** You position the cell pointer three rows from the bottom and create horizontal windows. ◀

Press	↑ twice	Moves to A38.
Press	/, W, W, H	Selects Worksheet, Window, Horizontal.
Press	F6, ↓ six times	Shifts to bottom window in C38; moves to monthly total row.

The monthly totals are now visible in the lower window.

Press	F6	Shifts to upper window in C37.

You move up column C, checking subtotals. Note the subtotals add up to half of the totals. The data is now being added twice in the monthly total. You move to the Jan total formula in C44 in the bottom window. You build a correct formula, adding the subtotals. You use the windows to facilitate the pointing process.

Press	F5	
Type	C41 ↵ENTER	Moves to CENTRAL Subtotal, C41.

This will be the first cell in the formula, so place the cell pointer there.

Press	F6	Moves to C44 in bottom window.
Press	+, F6	Starts the formula; points to C41 in upper window.
Press	+	Returns to C44 in bottom window.

The formula is now +C41+.

Press	F6, ↑ nine times	Points to SOUTH subtotal, C32, in upper window.
Press	+, F6, ↑ nine times	Includes WEST subtotal, C23, in formula.

Press	(+), (F6), (↑) nine times, (↵ ENTER)	Includes NORTH subtotal, C14, in formula; enters the formula.

The correct formula for Jan totals is in C44. Copy the formula to the other month and the row total column.

Press	(/), (C), (↵ ENTER)	Selects Copy with Copy what? range C44.
Press	(→), (.), (END), (→), (↵ ENTER)	Copies formula to D44..O44.

After clearing the windows, the worksheet should look like Figure 13.1.

Figure 13.1 *Revenue by Month*

ACE HARDWARE
1991 DETAILED REVENUE FORECAST
(in thousands)

PRODUCT	REGION	JAN	FEB	MARCH	APRIL	MAY	JUNE	JULY	AUG	SEPT	OCT	NOV	DEC	TOTAL
BOLTS	NORTH	4.8	6.4	5.6	8.8	8.0	10.4	4.0	4.8	7.2	4.8	6.4	8.8	80.0
NAILS	NORTH	3.0	4.0	3.5	5.5	5.0	6.5	2.5	3.0	4.5	3.0	4.0	5.5	50.0
NUTS	NORTH	3.6	4.8	4.2	6.6	6.0	7.8	3.0	3.6	5.4	3.6	4.8	6.6	60.0
SCREWS	NORTH	6.0	8.0	7.0	2.4	10.0	1.0	5.0	6.0	9.0	6.0	8.0	11.0	79.4
WASHERS	NORTH	2.4	3.2	2.8	1.2	4.0	2.0	2.0	2.4	3.6	2.4	3.2	4.4	33.6
MISCELLANEOUS	NORTH	1.2	1.6	1.4	2.4	2.0	1.3	1.0	1.2	1.8	1.2	1.6	2.2	18.9
Subtotal		21.0	28.0	24.5	26.9	35.0	29.0	17.5	21.0	31.5	21.0	28.0	38.5	321.9
BOLTS	WEST	2.4	3.2	2.8	1.2	4.0	1.5	2.0	2.4	3.6	2.4	3.2	4.4	33.1
NAILS	WEST	1.2	2.0	1.8	1.8	2.5	2.5	1.3	1.5	2.3	1.5	2.0	2.8	23.2
NUTS	WEST	1.8	2.4	2.1	3.0	3.0	1.0	1.5	1.8	2.7	1.8	2.4	3.3	26.8
SCREWS	WEST	3.0	4.0	3.5	1.2	5.0	0.5	2.5	3.0	4.5	3.0	4.0	5.5	39.7
WASHERS	WEST	1.2	1.6	1.4	0.6	2.0	2.6	1.0	1.2	1.8	1.2	1.6	2.2	18.4
MISCELLANEOUS	WEST	0.6	0.8	0.7	3.6	1.0	1.3	0.5	0.6	0.9	0.6	0.8	1.1	12.5
Subtotal		10.2	14.0	12.3	11.4	17.5	9.4	8.8	10.5	15.8	10.5	14.0	19.3	153.7
BOLTS	SOUTH	3.6	4.8	4.2	2.1	6.0	7.8	3.0	3.6	5.4	3.6	4.8	6.6	55.5
NAILS	SOUTH	2.1	3.0	2.6	2.4	3.8	4.9	1.9	2.3	3.4	2.3	3.0	4.1	35.8
NUTS	SOUTH	2.4	3.6	3.2	4.2	4.5	5.9	2.3	2.7	4.1	2.7	3.6	5.0	44.2
SCREWS	SOUTH	4.2	6.0	5.3	1.8	7.5	9.8	3.8	4.5	6.8	4.5	6.0	8.3	68.5
WASHERS	SOUTH	1.8	2.4	2.1	0.6	3.0	3.9	1.5	1.8	2.7	1.8	2.4	3.3	27.3
MISCELLANEOUS	SOUTH	0.6	1.2	1.1	1.6	1.5	2.0	0.8	0.9	1.4	0.9	1.2	1.7	14.9
Subtotal		14.7	21.0	18.5	12.7	26.3	34.3	13.3	15.8	23.8	15.8	21.0	29.0	246.2
BOLTS	CENTRAL	1.2	1.6	1.4	0.8	2.0	2.6	1.0	1.2	1.8	1.2	1.6	2.2	18.6
NAILS	CENTRAL	0.6	1.0	0.9	1.4	1.3	1.6	0.6	0.8	1.1	0.8	1.0	1.4	12.5
NUTS	CENTRAL	0.6	1.2	1.1	1.7	1.5	2.0	0.8	0.9	1.4	0.9	1.2	1.7	15.0
SCREWS	CENTRAL	1.2	2.0	1.8	2.8	2.5	3.3	1.3	1.5	2.3	1.5	2.0	2.8	25.0
WASHERS	CENTRAL	0.6	0.8	0.7	1.1	1.0	1.3	0.5	0.6	0.9	0.6	0.8	1.1	10.0
MISCELLANEOUS	CENTRAL	0.0	0.4	0.4	0.6	0.5	0.7	0.3	0.3	0.5	0.3	0.4	0.6	5.0
Subtotal		4.2	7.0	6.3	8.4	8.8	11.5	4.5	5.3	8.0	5.3	7.0	9.8	86.1
		=====	=====	=====	=====	=====	=====	=====	=====	=====	=====	=====	=====	=====
MONTHLY TOTAL		50.1	70.0	61.6	59.4	87.6	84.2	44.1	52.6	79.1	52.6	70.0	96.6	807.9

Clear the windows and save the worksheet.

Press	/, W, W, C	Selects Worksheet, Window, Clear.
Press	/, F, S	Selects File, Save.
Type	REVMH132 ↵ENTER	Saves worksheet under REVMH132.

PROCEDURE SUMMARY

VIEWING TITLES

To set titles:

Move the cell pointer to the right of the last column and/or below the last row in the title(s).	
Activate the Main menu.	/
Select Worksheet.	W
Select Titles.	T
Select Vertical, Horizontal, or Both.	V, H, or B

To cancel titles:

Activate the Main menu.	/
Select Worksheet.	W
Select Titles.	T
Select Clear.	C

USING WINDOWS

To divide the screen into two windows:

Position the cell pointer on the screen where you want the top or the left edge of the second window to be.	
Activate the Main menu.	/
Select Worksheet.	W
Select Window.	W
Select Horizontal or Vertical.	H or V

To set the scrolling option:

Activate the Main menu.	/
Select Worksheet.	W
Select Window.	W
Select Sync or Unsync.	S or U

To cancel the windows:

Activate the Main menu.	/
Select Worksheet.	W
Select Window.	W
Select Clear.	C

To move between windows:

Press	F6

EXERCISES

13A In this exercise, you modify the large worksheet from the end of the tutorial.

1. Retrieve the REVMH132 file.
2. Right align the text "First" in cell P4.
3. Right align the text "6 Months" in cell P5.
4. Right align the text "Second" in cell Q4.
5. Right align the text "6 Months" in cell Q5.
6. Copy the underlinings in cell O6 to cells P6 and Q6.
7. Set the column width of columns P and Q to 10.

   In exercises 8 through 11, with the vertical windows in Synchronize mode, build the formulas using pointing and copying.
8. In the corresponding row of column P, determine the total revenues for the first six months for each product in each region.
9. In the corresponding row of column Q, determine the total revenues for the second six months for each product in each region.
10. Place single underlinings in cells P13, Q13, P22, Q22, P31, Q31, P40, and Q40 and double underlinings in cells P43 and Q43.
11. Compute the subtotal revenue for each region for the first six months and second six months of the year.

12. Compute the total revenue for all products and regions for the first six months and second six months of the year.
13. Use unsynchronized windows to see the effect on the overall total of doubling the revenue for Bolts in each region.
14. Clear the windows.
15. Save the worksheet using the filename E13A.
16. Print the worksheet.

13B In this exercise, you modify an existing worksheet.

1. Retrieve the E12B file.
2. Divide the worksheet area into two synchronized horizontal windows at row 14.
3. In the upper window, set row 6 as a horizontal title and column A as a vertical title.
4. Set column A as a vertical title in the lower window.
5. Move between and around the two windows.
6. Change the growth rates for Dryers to 1.9%, 2.1%, and 2.1% in the lower window and see the change in sales in the upper window.
7. Clear the windows and clear the titles.
8. Save the worksheet using the filename E13B.

Additional Printing Capabilities

CONCEPTS In addition to the basic printing capabilities (discussed in Topic 5), 1-2-3 provides additional facilities that help you create more readable and informative reports, assist with printing large worksheets, and help you understand and document your worksheets. These facilities are accessed through the Options command in the Print menu. Some of these options are described in Table 14.1. Header, Footer, and Borders are discussed in detail in the next section.

Table 14.1
Print Options

Option	Use
Header	Defines a header that appears below the top margin of each printed page.
Footer	Defines a footer that appears above the bottom margin of each printed page.
Margins	Establishes the top, bottom, and side margins.
Borders	Specifies rows and columns that will appear at the top of and to the left of every printed page.
Setup	Establishes sequences of characters that are used to control special features of the printer.
Pg-Length	Sets the number of lines on the page.

Selecting the Options command from the Print menu brings up another menu called the **Print Options menu**. When you complete a command that started in this menu, 1-2-3 returns you to the menu again so that you can select other options. Selecting Quit returns you to the Print menu.

Printing Headers and Footers

157

> **TIP** You may also erase the contents of the header and footer by using the Clear All sequence from the Print menu.

The Header and Footer options allow you to define a single line of text that will display at the top and bottom of each report page, respectively. 1-2-3 leaves two blank lines between the main text and the header or footer. When you select one of these options, 1-2-3 displays any previous header or footer and puts you in Edit mode. If no header or footer is defined, type in your text. If one is defined, you may edit the existing text or press the ESCAPE key to erase it and then enter the new text.

Most text entered into the header or footer displays as you have type it. However, Table 14.2 describes four special characters that you can include in headers and footers to provide special capabilities.

Table 14.2
Special Characters for Headers and Footers

Character	Use
@	Indicates where the date is to be printed.
#	Indicates where the page number is to be printed.
¦	Splits the header into left-justified, centered, and right-justified segments.
\	When placed as the first character and followed by a cell address, specifies that the contents of the cell should be used as the header or footer.

For example, entering " @ ¦ ABC ¦ Page # " as a header causes the date to be printed left justified, the company name ABC to be printed centered, and the page number to be printed right justified on the top of each page of the report. The header or footer is included only on the printout; there is no change in the worksheet area. To see the header or footer without printing out the report, you choose the option or check the Print Settings sheet.

Printing Borders 157

Borders provide capabilities in printing similar to those that Titles provide in viewing information on the screen. The Borders options allow you to specify a range of rows that will appear at the top of each printed page and a range of columns that will appear at the left side of each printed page.

> **TIP** When you specify your print range, you should not include the border rows or columns since they will then be printed twice, once in the border and then again in the print range.

Consider the following typical application of borders. You have a large table of information that requires many pages to print. At the top of the table are rows of labels that describe the column contents. For printing purposes, you select Borders Row and then specify a range of cells containing the rows of labels at the top of the table. The columns you specify are not important. When 1-2-3 prints the report, data from these rows appears at the top of each page. The columns printed from these rows will be the same as the columns selected for the print range. Similarly, column borders are used to print user-selected columns on each page if your report is too wide to fit on a single page. ◀

To remove borders once they have been established, you use the Clear Borders or Clear All command available in the Print menu.

Using the Page Break Command 158

In large worksheets, you can let the length of the page determine where the page breaks occur by printing the entire range. 1-2-3 fits as many rows as it can on a page and then moves to the next page. You also can control page breaks by printing a series of print ranges and using the Page command to move to a new page after each range. Although the latter method gives you control over where page breaks occur, it can be time consuming and may lead to erroneously skipping rows or to printing some rows twice.

> **TIP** You do not need to use the /Worksheet Page command to enter the page break label. If there is a blank line where you want to put the page break, you can type the page break label into this row in the first column of the print range.

Using the /Worksheet Page command is a much easier method that has essentially the same result. To use this command, position the cell pointer in the first column of the print range on a row that is to start a new page. You then execute the command. 1-2-3 inserts a blank row in your worksheet (essentially using /Worksheet Insert Row) and puts a label into the current cell. Examining the current cell contents, you see that the cell contains the **page break label** ¦::, the split vertical bar (¦) followed by two colons (::). As discussed in Topic 3, the split vertical bar is a label prefix that 1-2-3 uses to indicate labels containing information for printing. Data in cells to the right of the page break label does not print. ◀

If you change your worksheet and need to modify the pagination, you can remove the page break label by deleting the entire row, erasing the label, or replacing it with something else. Note, however, that if you do erase it, a new blank row appears in the output report.

TUTORIAL

In this tutorial, you learn additional methods for enhancing your reports. These techniques are headers, footers, borders, and page breaks. You should have the REVMH131 worksheet from the last topic on the screen. Position the cell pointer in cell C7.

1 **Define headers and footers.** Headers or footers are printed on the top or bottom of each page. First, define headers.

Press	/, P, P	Selects Print, Printer.
Press	O, H	Selects Options, Header.

The message "Enter header:" is on the control panel. You now type in your header line.

Type	¦ ACE HARDWARE - MONTHLY FORECAST ¦@	
Press	↵ ENTER	Locks in header.

The ¦ separates the header into sections. The @ symbol is replaced by the date. The header appears in the Print Settings sheet. Now you enter a footer.

Press	F	Selects Footer.

The message "Enter footer:" is on the control panel.

Type	A:\REVMH131 ¦ Page #	
Press	↵ ENTER	Locks in footer.

The footer prints the worksheet filename in the lower left corner of each page. It prints "Page N." centered on the bottom of the *N*th page since the symbol # is replaced by the page numbers. It appears in the Print Settings sheet.

2 **Define borders.** Borders have the same relationship with the printout that titles have with the screen. Borders appear on the top and left sides of each page in the report. Therefore they enable you to have column and row headings appear on each page of the report.

Press	B, R	Selects Borders, Rows.

The message "Enter range for border rows: C7" is on the control panel. You highlight any cell in the rows you want to use as the borders. You choose the month names and the underlinings as row borders. You choose the product and region names as column borders.

Press	↑ twice, ., ↓, ↵ENTER	Selects rows 5 and 6 as border rows; returns to Print Options menu.
Press	B, C	Selects Borders, Columns.

The message "Enter range for border columns: C7" is on the control panel.

Press	←, ., ←, ↵ENTER	Selects columns A and B as border columns.

Borders are displayed in the Print Settings sheet.

Press	Q, Q	Selects Quit, Quit.

Leaves the Print Options menu and then the Print menu.

3 **Set page break.** The Page Break option allows to determine where new pages will begin. You put one after each region so that each region is printed on its own page. You put them in Column C since this is the first column of the print range. First, you insert a page break after the North region.

Move to	C13	
Press	/, W, P	Selects Worksheet, Page.

The :: symbol appears in cell C13. The current cell contents are ¦ ::. Now put page breaks between the other regional groups.

Press	↓ six times, /, W, P	Moves to C20; selects Worksheet, Page.
Press	↓ six times, /, W, P	Moves to C27; selects Worksheet, Page.
Press	↓ eight times, /, W, P	Moves to C36; selects Worksheet, Page.

You now have page breaks after each regional group. There is also one at the end of the range so that when the printing is done, 1-2-3 moves to the top of the next page.

4 **Print the report.** You now print out the report to see the effect of the various choices that you have made. Make sure that the paper is at the top of a page and that the printer is on line.

Press	/, P, P	Selects Print, Printer.

You should check the Print Settings display now to verify that the settings are correct. For the print range, you highlight from Jan for BOLTS in the NORTH, C7, through the blank below overall total, O36. This includes the final page break.

Press	R	Selects Range.
Move to	C7	
Press	., END, ↓, ↑	
Press	END, →, ↓, ↵ENTER	Moves to O36; highlights print range C7..O36.
Press	A, G	Selects Align, Go; prints report.

Note the paging, borders, headers, and footers.

Press	Q	Selects Quit; leaves Print menu.
Press	/, F, S	Selects File, Save.
Type	REVMH14 ↵ENTER	Saves worksheet under REVMH14.

PROCEDURE SUMMARY

DEFINING HEADERS AND FOOTERS

Access the Print Options menu.	/, P, P, O
Select Header or Footer.	H or F
Type the information.	(your input)
Enter the input.	↵ENTER
Leave the Print Options menu.	Q

DEFINING BORDERS

Position the cell pointer in the first column or row in the border.	
Access the Print Options menu.	/, P, P, O

Select Borders.	B
Highlight any row in border column(s) or any column in border row(s).	(pointer-movement keys or mouse)
Lock in the selection.	↵ ENTER
Leave the Print Options menu.	Q

USING THE PAGE BREAK COMMAND

Position the cell pointer in the first column of the print range in the row where the new page starts.	
Activate the Main menu.	/
Select Worksheet.	W
Select Page.	P

EXERCISES

14A In this exercise, you print a worksheet using a header, footer, borders, and page breaks.

1. Retrieve the E13A file.
2. Create a header with the text "Ace Hardware" centered and the date at the right side of the header.
3. Create a footer with the text "Confidential" centered and the page number at the right side of the footer.
4. Select rows 2 through 6 as border rows.
5. Select columns A and B as border columns.
6. Insert a page break in the row immediately after the subtotal revenue for each region.
7. Save the worksheet using the filename E14A.
8. Print only the data for the months January through June.

14B In this exercise, you print a worksheet using a header, footer, borders, and page breaks.

1. Retrieve the E13B file.
2. Select column A as a border column.
3. Select row 6 as a border row.
4. Create a header with the text "Able Appliance Co." centered and the page number at the right side of the header.
5. Create a footer with your name at the left side of the footer.
6. Insert a page break between the sales and the growth rates.
7. Save the worksheet using the filename E14B and print it.

Managing Data

CONCEPTS

Once you have entered information into a 1-2-3 worksheet, you can manipulate it in many ways. The name 1-2-3 itself addresses this issue, referring to the three major functions that the package supports: worksheet, data management, and graphics. (Topic 16 will discuss options for displaying information graphically.) This section discusses the /Data Sort and /Data Query commands, which provide capabilities for sorting tables of information and locating and selecting specific rows.

Organizing Data in 1-2-3

The data management commands apply to tables of data organized into rows and columns such as in the sales tracking worksheet shown in Figure 15.1. Each row, referred to as a **record**, contains the information describing a single sale. The items of information recorded for each sale (for example, the date, the amount, the person making the sale, and the customer) are organized into columns, called **fields**. All of the rows store the same category of information in the same column. At the top of the table you will find one or more rows of labels describing the column contents. You can use these rows as horizontal titles when you view the information or as row borders when you print it. You use one of these rows to provide the **field names**, which must be unique.

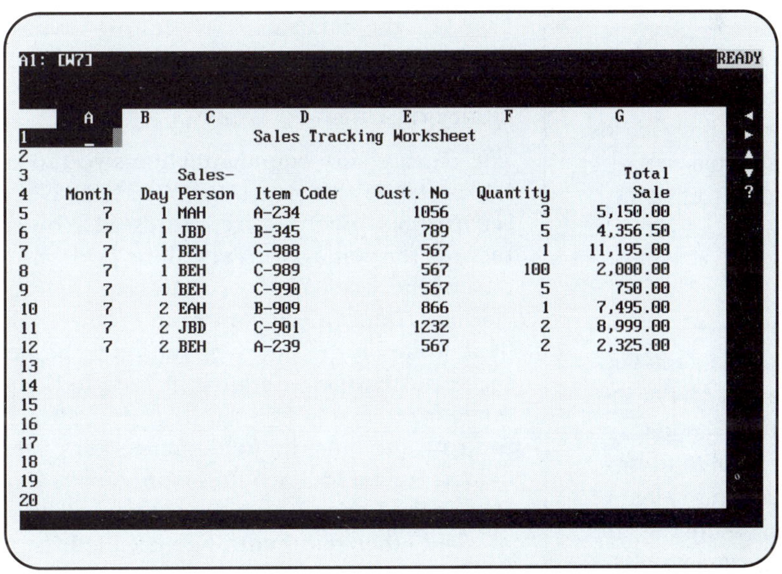

A1: [W7] READY

Sales Tracking Worksheet

	A	B	C	D	E	F	G
3			Sales-				Total
4	Month	Day	Person	Item Code	Cust. No	Quantity	Sale
5	7	1	MAH	A-234	1056	3	5,150.00
6	7	1	JBD	B-345	789	5	4,356.50
7	7	1	BEH	C-988	567	1	11,195.00
8	7	1	BEH	C-989	567	100	2,000.00
9	7	1	BEH	C-990	567	5	750.00
10	7	2	EAH	B-909	866	1	7,495.00
11	7	2	JBD	C-901	1232	2	8,999.00
12	7	2	BEH	A-239	567	2	2,325.00

Figure 15.1
Data Organized in a 1-2-3 Table

Sorting Tables of Data

168

The /Data Sort command is used to reorder the rows within a table. You can sort tables of sales transactions or expenses in different ways, for example, by date, department, or amount. Worksheets that contain forecasts of monthly revenues can be sorted alphabetically by revenue name, or numerically by revenue within a given month, by total revenues for the year, or by the difference between actual and budgeted revenues.

To sort data, you need to provide some information, including the range of data to be sorted, called the **data range**. 1-2-3 assumes that the information in this range is organized in a table. When you specify the data range, do *not* include the field names at the top of the range. Be careful to include all the rows to be sorted and, particularly, all the columns. ◀

> **TIP** The END, DOWN and END, RIGHT combinations are useful for pointing to the table of data that is completely filled in.

In addition to the data range, you must provide one column, called the **primary sort key**, to be used in determining the order in which the rows will be rearranged. A second column, called the **secondary sort key**, is optional. You specify the sort keys by pointing to any cell within the column. The cell need not be in the rows to be sorted.

For each sort key, you also specify the **sort order**, either ascending or descending. In ascending order, blanks come first, followed by labels, followed by values in increasing numerical order. Labels are sorted by the initial characters in the following order: blanks, numerals, letters in alphabetical order, and special characters. Columns sorted in descending order reverse the sequence.

The secondary sort key is used when the same value is found in multiple cells in the primary sort key. Those cells having the same primary key are further sorted based on the secondary key. ◀

> **TIP** If some of these cells have duplicate values for the secondary key also, the sort sequence of these cells cannot be predicted. In particular, you cannot assume they will be in the same relative position as in the initial table.

Once you have specified the data range and the sort keys, you use the Go option to perform the sort. 1-2-3 rearranges all rows in the data range based on the data values in the sort keys. Formulas in the table are adjusted as though they were being copied. ◀

> **TIP** As with any major change to your worksheet, it is a good idea to save the worksheet prior to sorting it.

Querying Data

168

The /Data Query command allows you to ask questions about your data tables. To do this, you supply certain selection **criteria** that determine the records in which you are interested. You can tell 1-2-3 to **find** these records for you, to **extract** all or portions of these records to a different area of the worksheet, or to **delete** the records from the original table.

The /Data Query command requires you to define two or three ranges, depending on the query operation to be performed. The first range, called the **input range**, contains the data to be queried. 1-2-3 assumes that this range is organized in a table (as described in the previous section) and its top row contains the field names. For example, an input range using the data in Figure 15.1 would begin in row 4 and include columns A through G. The field names would be the labels in row 4.

The other required range is called the **criteria range**. This range is used to store the rules by which 1-2-3 selects records in the input range. The range contains at least one column and at least two rows. The first row contains one or more field names drawn from the field names in the input range. ◀

> **TIP** The field names in the first row of the criteria range must be identical to those found in the input range. To ensure this, you can use the /Copy command to input the first row of the criteria range.

TIP When the cells below the field names are empty, 1-2-3 selects records having any value in those columns. Hence an empty row in the criteria range results in all the records being selected.

The second and following rows in the criteria range contain the selection criteria. 1-2-3 permits three types of criteria: criteria specifying an exact match, criteria specifying a pattern match in columns containing labels, and criteria specified by a relational or logical (true/false) formula.

If you include more than two rows in the criteria table, 1-2-3 regards each additional row as a separate set of selection criteria and selects rows that match any of the criteria. When a row contains values in two or more columns, all values must be found in any record selected.

To specify exact match, you enter the value that must be matched under the field name of the column in which the value must lie. ◀

In columns containing labels, you select records based on patterns in the labels. In specifying the patterns, 1-2-3 uses three special characters. The question mark (?) placed in the pattern indicates that any character is considered a match in that position. An asterisk (*) indicates that any character or group of characters may follow the text that precedes the asterisk. The tilde (~) placed at the front of a pattern excludes rather than accepts records that match the pattern. Thus the pattern "~A*" selects any item that does not begin with the letter A.

Finally, 1-2-3 uses formulas as criteria. These formulas allow you to select ranges of values or records that satisfy conditions based on other values in the records. To create these formulas, 1-2-3 uses other operations called **relational operations**. The symbols used to represent these operations and their meaning are shown in Table 15.1.

Table 15.1
Relational Operations

Symbols	Relationship
The following relational operations compare the value on their left with the value on their right to determine whether the relationship they express is true or false. They give the value 1 if the relationship is true and 0 if it is false.	
=	Equal to
<>	Not equal to
<	Less than
<=	Less than or equal to
>	Greater than
>=	Greater than or equal to

Formulas that are used for criteria should refer to the cell addresses in the first row of data in the table. They can be placed in any column in the criteria range. For example, if the first record is in row 5, entering the relation +G5>5000 in any column in the criteria range selects the records from the data range in which the entries in column G are greater than 5000.

Once you have specified the input and criteria ranges, you can use the two Query options, Find and Delete. The Find option locates records in the input range that satisfy the selection criteria. The Delete option removes the records in the input range that satisfy the criteria.

TIP To extract all the fields, copy the field names from the input range into another area in the worksheet and then define the output range to include all the field names.

TIP Be careful. 1-2-3 erases the rows below the first in the output range prior to extracting records. If you are using only a single row for the output range, 1-2-3 erases all the way to the bottom of the worksheet.

The other two Query options, Extract and Unique, take some or all of the fields in the records selected by the criteria and place them in another area on the worksheet. The fields that are to be extracted and where the information is placed are determined by an additional range called the **output range**. The output range consists of at least one row and one column. The first row contains the names of the fields you wish to have placed in that column. ◀

The number of rows in the output range determines the maximum number of rows that 1-2-3 can extract. If you include only the one row containing the field names in the output range, 1-2-3 uses the remainder of the worksheet below this row to hold extracted records. If you specify additional rows, 1-2-3 only extracts as many rows as can fit into the range you specify. ◀

The Unique option is similar to the Extract option except that Unique copies only the unique combinations of output fields that are present in the selected records. That is, if two or more selected records have the same values for all the fields in the output range, 1-2-3 copies only the first of these records.

TUTORIAL

In this tutorial, you learn how to sort information in the worksheet, alphabetizing selected columns or arranging data values in numerical order. You also learn how to extract information from one part of the worksheet to another part. You should have REVMH131 on the screen with columns A and B set as vertical titles; rows 5 and 6 as horizontal titles; a global format of one fixed decimal place; and a global column width of seven characters.

1 **Sort your data.** In this section, you sort the data in the worksheet to analyze it from different perspectives. You first must select the data range that includes all the rows containing input data and all the nonempty columns including row labels and formulas.

Press	HOME	Moves to C7.
Press	/, D, S	Selects Data, Sort.

The Sort Settings display overlays part of the worksheet area.

Press	D	Selects Data-Range.

The message "Enter data range: C7" is on the control panel. You select the range by pointing starting in A7, the first column of the first row in the table.

Press	← twice, .	Anchors cell pointer in A7.
Press	END, ↓, END, →, ↵ ENTER	Selects A7..O30 as data range; returns to Sort menu.

You now sort the rows in the data range alphabetically by product name.

Press	P	Selects Primary-key.

The message "Primary sort key: C7" is on the control panel. Because you want the product names in alphabetical order to determine the order of the rows, you select column A as the primary key and ascending order.

Press	END, ←, ↵ ENTER	Selects column A as primary key.

The message "SORT order (A or D): D" is on the control panel.

Type	A ↵ ENTER	Selects ascending order.
Press	G	Selects Go; sorts data range; returns to Ready mode.

TIP You can also check the data range or the primary key by pressing D or P, respectively. The current choice is highlighted on the screen and is on the control panel.

The data is now arranged with all the BOLTS rows first, all the MISCELLANEOUS rows next, and so on. Within each product category, the regions are in no particular order. You now alphabetize the regions within product category.

Press	/, D, S	Selects Data, Sort.

The program remembers the previously selected data range and primary key. See the Sort Settings screen. ◄

TIP The secondary key is still set. You can cancel all the sort settings by choosing Reset in the Sort menu. Although you cannot cancel only the secondary key, you can cancel its effect on the sort process by setting it equal to the primary key.

Press	S	Selects Secondary-key.

The message "Secondary sort key: C7" is on the control panel.

Press	←, ↵ ENTER	Selects column B.
Type	A ↵ ENTER	Selects ascending sort order.
Press	G	Selects Go; sorts data range.

The BOLTS rows are first, then the MISCELLANEOUS rows, and so on. Within each product block, the rows are arranged alphabetically by region. Next you sort by total revenue. ◄

Press	/, D, S, P	Selects Data, Sort, Primary.
Press	END, →, ↵ ENTER	Selects total column, O, as primary key.
Press	D, ↵ ENTER	Selects descending order.
Press	G	Selects Go; sorts data range.

The rows are ordered based on the values in the total revenue column, arranged in decreasing order. After any sort, you can save the sorted worksheet under the same or a different name. If you use a different name, you can return to the original order by retrieving the worksheet.

2 **Prepare to extract.** To have the extraction process work, you need to replace the underlinings at the top of the columns with the column headings. The column headings then are used as the field names.

Press	F5	
Type	A5 ↵ENTER	Moves to A5 in title area.
Press	/, C, END, →, ↵ENTER	Selects Copy with Copy what? range A5..O5.
Press	↓, ↵ENTER	Copies to row of underlinings, 6.

Note that with titles set, the column headings now appear on the screen four times. Delete the extra copy.

Press	/, W, D, R, ↵ENTER	Selects Worksheet, Delete, Row; deletes row 5.

To extract information from one range in the worksheet to another range, you first must set up an input range, a criteria range, and an output range. To follow the results of the extraction more easily, you change the titles and create a horizontal window.

Press	/, W, T, C	Selects Worksheet, Titles, Clear; removes current titles.
Press	HOME, ↓ nine times	Moves to A10.

You have positioned the cell pointer about halfway between the top and the bottom of the worksheet area.

Press	/, W, W, H	Selects Worksheet, Window, Horizontal.

You have created a horizontal window in the middle of the worksheet area. The cell pointer is in the upper window. Now you set the titles.

Press	↓ four times	Puts row 5 at top of screen.
Move to	C6	
Press	/, W, T, B	Selects Worksheet, Titles, Both.

You set columns A and B as vertical titles. You have set row 5 as a horizontal title. The titles are active only in the upper window. The cell pointer is in cell C6. You select the input range for the extraction. You move to the beginning of the field name row, 5. The input range goes from the label PRODUCT, A5, through the row total for MISCELLANEOUS - CENTRAL.

Press	F5	
Type	A5 ↵ENTER	Moves to A5 in title area.
Press	/, D, Q	Selects Data, Query.

The Query Settings display overlays part of the worksheet area.

Press	I	Selects Input.

The message "Enter the input range: A5" is on the control panel. Select the range by pointing.

Press	., END, ↓, END, →, ↵ENTER	Highlights and enters range A5..O29.

Now you switch to the bottom window and set the criteria and output ranges. You first copy the column headings for the ranges since they must match the field exactly.

Press	Q, F6	Leaves menu; switches to bottom window in A10.
Press	PAGE DOWN nine times, ↓	Moves to A101.

You copy the field names PRODUCT, REGION, and TOTAL from the upper window to A101..C101 in the lower window.

Press	/, C, ESC	Selects Copy; converts to cell address.
Press	F6, ↑, ←, .	Switches to C6 in upper window; anchors cell pointer in B5.
Press	←, ↵ENTER	Selects labels PRODUCT and REGION, A5..B5, as Copy what? range; returns to A101 in lower window.
Press	↵ENTER	Copies labels to A101..B101.
Press	→ twice	Moves to C101.
Press	/, C, ESC, F6, ↑	Selects Copy; moves to C5 in upper window.
Press	END, →, ↵ENTER, ↵ENTER	Copies TOTAL from O5 to C101.

You copy the labels from A101..C101 to A105..C105.

Press	← twice	Moves to A101.
Press	/, C, → twice, ↵ ENTER	Selects Copy with Copy what? range A101..C101.
Press	↓ four times, ↵ ENTER	Copies labels to A105..C105.

You choose the criteria range, A101..C102.

Press	/, D, Q, C	Selects Data, Query, Criteria.
Press	., → twice, ↓, ↵ ENTER	Selects criteria range.

You choose the output range, A105..C105.

Press	O, ↓ four times	Selects Output; moves to A105.
Press	., → twice, ↵ ENTER	Selects output range, A105..C105.
Press	Q	Selects Quit.

4 **Extract.** You perform four extractions, each of which is designed to illustrate a different type of criteria. The first criteria is a label match. You put the label to be matched in cell A102.

Press	↓	Moves to A102.
Type	BOLTS ↵ ENTER	Enters BOLTS in A102.
Press	/, D, Q, E	Selects Data, Query, Extract.

Information is extracted from the four rows in the input range for the product BOLTS and put in the output range. "Extraction" may be a misleading term here because the information is also left in its original location. The output range contains the values, not the formulas. The columns extracted are the ones whose headings were used as headings in the output range. The Query menu is still on the screen. The second extraction is based on a comparison of the total values to a constant. The comparison is entered as a formula. First, you erase the old criteria.

TIP It is very helpful here if you take advantage of the windows. It is sometimes easier to build the formula by pointing, using the WINDOW (F6) key to change windows.

Press	Q	Quit; returns to Ready mode.
Press	/, R, E, ↵ ENTER	Selects Range, Erase; erases contents of A102.
Press	→ twice	Moves to C102. ◀
Press	+, F6	Starts formula; moves to upper window.

Press	END, →	Moves to and enters O6 into formula.
Type	>40 ↵ENTER	Returns to C102 in lower window; enters formula into C102.

The criteria has been entered as a formula in cell C102, which displays 1 since the relation in the formula is true. Now perform the extraction.

Press	/, D, Q, E, Q	Selects Data, Query, Extract, Quit.

The seven records in which the total revenue is bigger than 40 are extracted. Check the extraction by looking at the original data in the upper window. The third extraction requires that the records satisfy both of two conditions, namely, that the product be BOLTS and that the total revenue be greater than 40. The conditions must be in the same row.

Press	← twice	Moves to A102.
Type	BOLTS ↵ENTER	Enters BOLTS in A102.

This time you perform the extraction without using the menu.

Press	F7	Performs the extraction.

The two records in which total revenue from BOLTS is greater than 40 are extracted. The last extraction requires that the records satisfy at least one of the two conditions set earlier. The conditions must be in different rows.

Press	/, M, ↵ENTER, ↓, ↵ENTER	Moves BOLTS from A102 to A103.

Because you have put part of the criteria for extraction in cell A103, you must include row 103 in the criteria range.

Press	/, D, Q, C	Selects Data, Query, Criteria.

The message "Enter criteria range: A101..C102" is on the control panel.

Press	↓, ↵ENTER	Changes criteria range to A101..C103.
Press	E, Q	Selects Extract, Quit.

The nine records in which either the product is BOLTS or the total revenue is greater than 40 are extracted. You return to Ready mode.

PROCEDURE SUMMARY

SORTING TABLES OF DATA

To select the range to be sorted:

Activate the Main menu.	/
Select Data.	D
Select Sort.	S
Select Data-Range.	D
Highlight the range.	(pointer-movement keys or mouse)
Lock in the selection.	↵ ENTER

To sort the range:

Activate the Main menu.	/
Select Data.	D
Select Sort.	S
Specify the Data-Range if not correct.	(your input)
Select Primary-key.	P
Move the cell pointer to any cell in the primary-key column.	(pointer-movement keys or mouse)
Lock in the selection.	↵ ENTER
Select Ascending or Descending.	A or D
Lock in the selection.	↵ ENTER
Select Secondary-key (optional).	S
Move the cell pointer to any cell in the secondary-key column.	(pointer-movement keys or mouse)
Lock in the selection.	↵ ENTER
Select Ascending or Descending.	A or D
Lock in the selection.	↵ ENTER
Select Go.	G

QUERYING DATA

To select the input, criteria, or output range:

Activate the Main menu.	/

Select Data.	D
Select Query.	Q
Select Input, Criteria, or Output.	I, C, or O
Highlight the range.	(pointer-movement keys or mouse)
Lock in the selection.	↵ ENTER

To extract data:

Activate the Main menu.	/
Select Data.	D
Select Query.	Q
Specify input, criteria, and/or output ranges if needed.	(your input)
Lock in the selection.	↵ ENTER
Select Extract.	E

EXERCISES

15A In this exercise, you create a worksheet, sort data, and extract data in the worksheet.

1. Create the following worksheet.

Able Appliance Company
Employees

Last Name	First Name	Region	Salary	Emp Num
Villanucci	Pat	1	31000	1
Thompson	Alice	2	30000	2
Jones	Tom	3	29000	3
Rodriguez	Al	2	25000	4
Jones	Robert	3	26000	5
Chen	James	2	27500	6
Walker	Jim	2	28500	7
Jones	Susan	1	29000	8
Jackson	Jim	1	27500	9
Thompson	John	3	30500	10

2. Save the worksheet using the filename E15A1.
3. Sort the worksheet by Salary in descending order.
4. Save the worksheet using the filename E15A2.
5. Sort the worksheet by last name and then first name.
6. Save the worksheet using the filename E15A3.
7. Retrieve the E15A1 file.

For each Query, extract the Last Name, First Name, Region, and Salary.

8. Set up the criteria range and output range below the worksheet starting in cell A21.
9. Use synchronized horizontal windows to view both the input data and the extracted data.
10. Extract the individuals having a salary less than 27,500.
11. Extract the individuals having a salary greater than 28,000.
12. Extract the individuals in region 3 having a salary less than 27,000.
13. Extract the individuals whose first name begins with J.
14. Extract the individuals whose first name or last name begins with J.
15. Save the worksheet using the filename E15A.
16. Print the worksheet including the extracted data on a separate page.

15B In this exercise, you sort data and extract data in an existing worksheet.

1. Retrieve the E12B file.
2. Sort the product data so that it is in alphabetical order by product.
3. Sort the growth rate assumption data so that it is in alphabetical order by product.

For each Query, extract the product name and 4th quarter data.

4. Set up the criteria range (starting in cell C21) and the output range (starting in cell C25). Use horizontal windows to view the input and extracted data.
5. Extract the products with total annual sales greater than 7000.
6. Extract the products with total annual sales greater than 7000 and 4th quarter sales greater than 3000.
7. Extract the products with total annual sales less than 6000 or 4th quarter sales less than 2000.
8. Save the worksheet using the filename E15B.
9. Print the worksheet including the extracted data on a separate page.

Using Graphs

TIP These graphs can also be printed using the PrintGraph facility available from the Lotus Access System menu.

CONCEPTS

For many types of numerical data, the relationships between the numbers are as important as the numbers themselves. For example, we may be interested in how sales and profit levels are changing with time. We may want to compare the sales in different product lines or sales territories.

Understanding such relationships from the numerical values themselves is often difficult. Because of their visual nature and the human ability to recognize and store visual patterns, graphs provide an effective alternative for examining these relationships. Therefore 1-2-3 allows you to create graphs from the information stored in your worksheet and to display the graphs on your screen. ◀

Defining a Graph

180

Graphs are defined using the /Graph command. When you select this command, 1-2-3 displays the **Graph Command menu** and replaces the worksheet area with the Graph Settings sheet. This sheet shows the current values of the ranges and options set through the graph commands. The graph described by these settings is called the **current graph**.

To create a graph, you need to select the graph type and at least one set of data to be graphed. You should also select the X-range. Table 16.1 shows the available graph types and gives a brief description of each.

Table 16.1
Graph Types

Type	Use
Line	Graphs the cell values in the data ranges A–F as sets of data points optionally displaying symbols at each point and connecting the points from the same data range by lines.
Bar	Represents the data values in the A–F ranges by vertical bars spaced uniformly along the x-axis.
XY	Creates a line graph with the horizontal positions of the data points determined by their associated X values.
Stacked-Bar	Displays data values as the lengths of vertical bars, stacking bars from different data ranges on top of one another.
Pie	Displays the A data range as the segments of a circle. Segments can be assigned optional colors or highlighting patterns and can be exploded.
HLCO	Creates a High-Low-Close-Open graph that allows investors in stocks and bonds to conveniently track prices of individual investments.
Mixed	Displays some data with a vertical bar and other data with lines.

All graph types, except for the pie chart and mixed graph, can plot up to six sets of data. The values to be used for the x-axis and the data sets are taken from rows or columns in the worksheet. You specify these ranges by selecting one of the commands X or A–F in the Graph menu and then pointing to the appropriate range. The ranges are displayed in the Graph Settings sheet as they are defined. Pie charts use the A range to define the size of each segment in the pie and the B range to shade the segments and optionally to explode them from the pie.

> **TIP** You can specify each of the ranges individually through the X and A–F commands. If the ranges are adjacent, the Group command allows you to specify all of them at once.

For all graph types except the XY graph, the X range provides descriptive information and may contain either labels or values. Pie charts display the entries in the X range next to the corresponding slices in the graph. Line, bar, and stacked-bar graphs place the entries in the X range uniformly along the bottom of the graph with the data points or bars positioned over them. In an XY graph, the X range must be defined. The cells in the range must contain numerical values, which determine the horizontal positions of the corresponding data points. 1-2-3 chooses the text along the horizontal axis. ◀

Once you have specified the data ranges required for your graph, you display it with the View command. The Graph Settings sheet and menu disappear, and 1-2-3 draws the graph on the screen. To return to the Graph Command menu, you press any key. When you are finished with your graph, you return to Ready mode by selecting the Quit option from the Graph menu. Saving the worksheet also saves the graph definition.

Enhancing the Graph (181)

In addition to the basic capabilities just discussed, 1-2-3 provides options that enhance the readability of your graphs. These features are available through the Options command, which displays the **Graph Options menu**. Table 16.2 shows some of the selections available from this menu, whose use is illustrated in the tutorial.

Table 16.2
Graph Options

Option	Use
Legend	Displays a legend at the bottom of the graph showing the color, pattern, or symbol used by each data series along with a description of the series.
Titles	Accepts input for up to two titles across the top of the graph and one each on the horizontal and vertical axes.
Grid	Controls the display of horizontal and vertical grid lines.
Scale	Controls the ranges of values and the displays along the vertical and horizontal axes.
Color	Specifies that the graph display is to be in color.
B&W	Specifies that the graph display is to be in monochrome.

> **TIP** Manual scaling is useful to ensure that different graphs use the same range of data values, to eliminate extreme data points, or to focus on a subset of the data.

For the Titles and Legend options you may use the text in a worksheet cell by typing \ followed by the cell address. 1-2-3 automatically selects the upper and lower limits on the y-axis. To override this automatic selection, you use the Scale option to specify that the scaling is to be manual. You then provide the upper and lower limits. ◀

Analyzing Changes Graphically

(181)

Once you have defined a graph, you can view it from Ready mode at any time by pressing the F10 function key called the **GRAPH key**. The graph display replaces the control panel and worksheet area just as it does when using the /Graph View command. If the data values in any of the ranges used by the graph have changed, the graph reflects these new values which allows you to examine modifications in your worksheet graphically. You return to Ready mode by pressing any key.

Naming Graphs

(181)

Frequently the data within a worksheet can provide information for many graphs. However, since only one graph can be current at any time, 1-2-3 allows you to store multiple graph definitions within a worksheet by naming graphs through the /Graph Name command. When you select this command, a menu displaying the selections shown in Table 16.3 appears.

Table 16.3
The /Graph Name Commands

Command	Use
Use	Activates a named graph.
Create	Assigns a name to the active graph and stores it as a named graph with that name.
Delete	Deletes the name and definition of a named graph.
Reset	Erases all graph names and their definitions.
Table	Displays a table showing all names graphs and the first title for the graph.

TIP Be careful when you use a named graph. The settings for the current graph are replaced by those of the named graph without warning.

To create a named graph, you select the /Graph Name Create command and supply a name of up to 15 characters. The settings for the current graph are stored under that name. You can then create additional graphs by modifying the current graph or starting over. For example, the current graph might use a bar graph to display the data. You could name this graph "BAR," then change the type to stacked-bar and name the new graph "SBAR." The /Graph Name Use command allows you to make a previously named graph the current graph. ◀

1-2-3 then displays the named graph on the screen using the current data values in the worksheet. To change a named graph, you first make it the current graph. Then you modify the current graph via the graph commands and options. The changes made to the current graph are not automatically transferred to the named graph. You must use the /Graph Name Create command again and specify the same name to store the graph. As with the current graph, all named graph definitions are stored when you save the worksheet.

> **TIP** Unless you have a color printer, be sure that the B&W graph option is in effect to take advantage of the hatching patterns 1-2-3 uses in bar and pie graphs.

Saving Graphs

182

To print graphs, you use the PrintGraph utility that is contained in your 1-2-3 package. This facility prints graphs that have previously been saved in special graph files through the /Graph Save command. To use the PrintGraph utility, you first store the specifications and data for the graph in a special file called a graph file. You create this file using the /Graph Save command, supplying 1-2-3 with the name to be given to the graph file. 1-2-3 creates the graph file from the current graph. Graph files are given the extension .PIC so that the PrintGraph utility can identify them. ◀

Accessing the PrintGraph Utility

182

You may access the PrintGraph utility by selecting the PrintGraph option from the Access System menu or by running the Pgraph program directly. When you enter the PrintGraph facility, the main PrintGraph menu appears along with the PrintGraph Settings sheet. PrintGraph also has an integrated, context-sensitive Help facility.

Setting the Options for Printing a Graph

The Settings command establishes all of the options that PrintGraph uses. Table 16.4 lists these options and briefly describes their purpose.

Table 16.4
The Settings Options

Option	Use
Image	Defines the size, font, and colors to be used in printing.
Hardware	Specifies where the graph files are located and other physical characteristics of your system.
Action	Controls printer actions between graphs.
Save	Saves the current settings permanently.
Reset	Retrieves the settings last saved with the Save command and makes them current.
Quit	Returns to the main PrintGraph menu.

As you use these options, your input is displayed in the PrintGraph Settings sheet. The settings you establish through these options apply only to the current session. To save them for future sessions, you use the Settings Save command, which updates a PrintGraph configuration file stored on disk. The Settings commands provide extensive flexibility in controlling how graphs will be printed and in describing your equipment.

Selecting and Viewing the Graphs to Print

You use the Image-Select option to specify the graph files to be printed. The names come from files with the .PIC extension in the Graphs Directory displayed in the PrintGraph Settings sheet.

> **TIP** To examine a graph on the screen prior to selection, you highlight the name and press the GRAPH (F10) key.

To select graphs to print, you highlight the names using the usual vertical movement keys and press the SPACEBAR. 1-2-3 places the # symbol in front of each graph selected. Although you cannot see it, the sequence in which you select the graphs is also retained and this is the sequence in which they will print. ◀

Printing Graphs

(182)

Once you have selected the graphs to be printed using Image-Select, you use the Go command to begin printing. It is a good idea to adjust the paper in your printer and then use the Align command to ensure that the program knows you are at the top of the page. To interrupt printing, you can use the CONTROL-BREAK key combination.

TUTORIAL

In this tutorial, you learn to create, use, save, and print some simple graphs. For these graphs you use information from the first three products in the REV12 worksheet. To begin the tutorial, therefore, you should have the REV12 worksheet on the screen.

1 Define a graph. In this section, you learn how to create a basic graph using the data for the products BOLTS, NAILS, and NUTS. You start with a bar graph. The cell pointer should be close to the data to be graphed.

Move to	B7	
Press	/, G	Selects Graph.

The Graph Settings display is on the screen.

Press	T, B	Selects Type, Bar; returns to Graph menu.

In the settings sheet, the type is Bar. Next you select the categories, Prior and Plan Revenue, for the x-axis (horizontal axis). Then you choose the data to be graphed for the three products.

Press	X	Selects X-range.

The message "Enter x-axis range: B7" is on the control panel. 1-2-3 suggests a cell address, which makes it easy to move to the desired range. You highlight the range containing the words PRIOR and PLAN, B4..C4.

Press	↑ three times	Points to PRIOR, B4.
Press	., →, ↵ENTER	Selects B4..C4 as x-axis range.

B4..C4 appears as the X-range in the Graph Settings sheet.

Press	A	Selects A, first data range.

The message "Enter first data range: B7" is on the control panel. A similar message will appear for the next two data ranges. In each case, you choose the prior and plan revenue values for the appropriate product.

Press	[.], [→], [↵ ENTER]	Selects revenue for BOLTS, B7..C7, as first data range.
Press	[B], [↓], [.], [→], [↵ ENTER]	Selects revenue for NAILS, B8..C8, as second data range, B.
Press	[C], [↓] twice, [.], [→], [↵ ENTER]	Selects revenue for NUTS, B9..C9, as third data range, C.

Any time you are in the Graph menu, you can view the current graph with its latest settings.

Press	[V]	Selects View.

The graph is drawn on the screen with its current settings and data. Note, at this point, that the graph is unclear because the meaning of the bars is not clear. In the next task, you enhance the graph to make it more understandable.

Press	[SPACEBAR]	Returns to Graph menu.

You can press any key to return to the Graph menu. You will now see how easy it is to change graph types.

TIP You can view the current graph at any time by pressing the GRAPH (F10) key.

Press	[T], [S], [V]	Selects Type, Stack-Bar, View.

The graph is now drawn as a stacked-bar graph. The bars representing the revenue for each product within a year are now placed on top of one another. Note that the graph uses the same settings and data as the previously drawn bar graph. 1-2-3 remembers and uses the most recent settings and data in drawing graphs under the View option. ◀

Press	[SPACEBAR]	Returns to Graph menu.
Press	[T], [B]	Selects Type, Bar; returns to original graph.

2 **Enhance the graph.** In this section, you add titles, legends, and a grid to the graph to make it more informative. First, you put a two-line title on the graph and a title on the y-axis (vertical axis).

Press	[O], [T], [F]	Selects Options, Titles, First.

The message "Enter first line of graph title:" is on the control panel.

Type	ACE HARDWARE [↵ ENTER]	Enters first title line.

"ACE HARDWARE" is displayed as the first title in the settings sheet. Note that you stay in the Graph Options menu.

Press	[T], [S]	Selects Titles, Second.
Type	1991 Revenue Forecast [↵ ENTER]	Enters second title line.
Press	[T], [Y]	Selects Titles, Y-axis.
Type	REVENUE [↵ ENTER]	Enters y-axis title.

Return to the Graph menu to view the graph.

Press	[Q], [V]	Selects Quit, View; draws graph on screen.
Press	[SPACEBAR]	Returns to Graph menu.

You add legends to the graph. Legends identify which bars go with which products.

Press	[O], [L], [R]	Options, Legends, Range.

The message "Enter legend range B7:" is on the control panel.

Press	[←], [.], [↓] twice, [↵ ENTER]	Selects BOLTS to NUTS, A7..A9, as legends.

The symbol "\A7" is listed as the first legend on the settings screen. Therefore, the first legend is the label in cell A7. The other two legends are similar. Now you view the graph again.

Press	[Q], [V]	Selects Quit, View.
Press	[SPACEBAR]	Returns to Graph menu.

Having viewed the graph with the legends assigned, you finally add a grid. A grid makes it easier to read the revenue values from the graph.

Press	[O], [G], [H]	Options, Grid, Horizontal.

Before viewing the graph, check the Graph Settings display.

Press	[Q], [V]	Selects Quit, View.
Press	[SPACEBAR], [Q]	Returns to Graph menu, then to Ready mode.

3 **Analyze data changes with a graph.** Change the revenue values in two of the cells from data ranges A and B. You then view the impact of these changes on the graph using the GRAPH (F10) key.

Move to	C7	
Type	180 (↓)	Enters 180; moves to C8.
Type	140 (↵ ENTER)	Enters 140.
Press	(F10)	Draws graph.

Note that the changes in the revenue values are reflected in the graph.

Press	(SPACEBAR)	Returns to worksheet.

4 **Name the graph.** If you save the worksheet, the most recently defined graph is also saved. Naming graphs allows you to store more than one graph with the worksheet.

Press	(/), (G), (N), (C)	Selects Graph, Name, Create.

The prompt "Enter graph name:" is on the control panel.

Type	Prior/Plan Bar (↵ ENTER)	Creates the named graph Prior/Plan Bar.

The current graph settings are saved under the name Prior/Plan Bar. You now define a new graph by changing the graph type. You save its settings under a different graph name.

Press	(T), (S), (V)	Selects Type, Stack-Bar, View.

The stacked-bar graph is drawn on the screen using the current settings.

Press	(SPACEBAR)	Returns to Graph menu.
Press	(N), (C)	Selects Name, Create.
Type	Prior/Plan Sbar (↵ ENTER)	Creates the named graph Prior/Plan Sbar.

The current graph settings are saved under the name Prior/Plan Sbar. You save the worksheet, which now includes the two graphs.

Press	(Q)	Selects Quit; leaves Graph menu.
Press	(/), (F), (S)	Selects File, Save.
Type	REV16 (↵ ENTER)	Saves worksheet under REV16.

5 **Save a graph.** Before printing a graph, you must create a graph file. You now create graph files for the two named graphs.

Press	/, G, N, U	Selects Graph, Name, Use.
Highlight	Prior/Plan Bar	
Press	↵ENTER	Makes Prior/Plan Bar the current graph; displays it.
Press	SPACEBAR	Returns to Graph menu.
Press	S	Selects Save.

The message "Enter graph file name A:\" is on the control panel.

Type	REVBAR ↵ENTER	Saves graph under REVBAR.

You now make the stacked bar graph the current graph.

Press	N, U	Selects Name, Use.
Highlight	Prior/Plan Sbar	
Press	↵ENTER	Makes Prior/Plan Sbar the current graph; displays it.
Press	SPACEBAR, S	Returns to Graph menu; selects Save.

The message "Enter graph file name: A:*.PIC" is on the control panel. Because there is already a graph file on the disk, the prompt now includes *.PIC.

Type	REVSBAR ↵ENTER	Saves graph under REVSBAR.
Press	Q	Selects Quit.

6 **Print the graph.** You print the graph REVSBAR. You use the PrintGraph option from the Access menu.

Press	/, Q, Y	Selects Quit, Yes.

This assumes you entered 1-2-3 by typing "Lotus". Then the Access menu is on the screen. If you entered 1-2-3 by typing "123", you must type "pgraph" at the DOS prompt to enter the PrintGraph utility.

Press	P	Selects PrintGraph.

The PrintGraph menu is onscreen. You select the graph(s) you want to print with the Image-Select option.

Press	I	Selects Image-Select.

Highlight	REVSBAR	
Press	SPACEBAR	Selects REVSBAR to print.

A # appears in front of REVSBAR.

Press	↵ ENTER	Locks in selection.

Be sure that the printer is turned on and positioned at the top of a page.

Press	A, G	Selects Align, Go; prints the graph.

The mode indicator displays *WAIT* and continues to display *WAIT* until the graph is finished printing.

Press	P	Selects Page.

Page moves the printer to the top of the next page. Finally, you leave the PrintGraph menu, 1-2-3, and the book.

Press	E, Y	Selects Exit, Yes.

If you entered 1-2-3 through the Access menu, you must exit from 1-2-3.

Press	E	Selects Exit; returns to DOS.

PROCEDURE SUMMARY

DEFINING A GRAPH

Activate the Main menu.	/
Select Graph.	G
Select Type.	T
Choose the type for the graph.	(your choice)
Select the X-range (optional, depending on type).	X
Specify the range.	(your input)
Lock in the selection.	↵ ENTER
Select data ranges. Include as many (up to six) as you need, depending on the type of graph and the data being graphed. Select data ranges in the same way the X-range was.	
When the data ranges have been selected, view the graph.	V
Return to the Graph menu.	(any key)
Leave the Graph menu.	Q

ENHANCING THE GRAPH

To define titles:

Access the Graph Option menu.	/, G, O
Select Titles.	T
Select the category of title.	(your choice)
Type the text for the title.	(your input)
Enter input.	↵ ENTER

To define legends:

Access the Graph Option menu.	/, G, O
Select Legends.	L
Select the data range for the legend.	(your choice)
Type the text for the legend.	(your input)
Enter input.	↵ ENTER

To create a grid:

Access the Graph Option menu.	/, G, O
Select Grid.	G
Select Horizontal or Vertical.	H or V

ANALYZING CHANGES GRAPHICALLY

Change some data in a data range in the worksheet.	
View the modified graph.	F10
Return to the worksheet.	(any key)

NAMING GRAPHS

To name a graph:

Access the Graph menu.	/, G
Select Name.	N
Select Create.	C
Type the desired name.	(your input)
Enter input.	↵ ENTER
Leave the Graph menu.	Q

To reactivate a graph:

Access the Graph menu.	/, G
Select Name.	N
Select Use.	U
Type or highlight the desired name.	(your input)
Enter input.	↵ ENTER

SAVING THE GRAPH

Activate the Main menu.	/
Select Graph.	G
Select Save.	S
Type or highlight the graph filename.	(your input)
Enter input.	↵ ENTER

ACCESSING THE PRINTGRAPH UTILITY

To access the PrintGraph menu from a worksheet:

Activate the Main menu.	/
Select Quit.	Q
Select Yes.	Y
Select PrintGraph.	P

PRINTING A GRAPH

To print a graph starting from the PrintGraph menu:

Select Image-Select.	I
Highlight the name of a graph you want to print.	(arrow keys)
Lock in the selection.	SPACEBAR
Return to the menu after selecting all the graphs to be printed.	↵ ENTER
Select Align.	A
Select Go.	G

EXERCISES

16A In this exercise, you create, save, and print two graphs.

1. Retrieve the E13A file.
2. Specify that the type of graph is pie.
3. Define the X data range as the product names in cells A7 through A12.
4. Designate the first data range (A) as the revenue numbers in cells C7 through C12.
5. Title the graph "1991 January Revenue."
6. View the graph.
7. Subtitle the graph "North Region."
8. View the graph.
9. Name the graph PIEGRAPH.
10. Save the graph using the graph filename PIEGRAPH.
11. Change the type to a bar graph.
12. View the graph.
13. Name the graph BARGRAPH.
14. Save the graph using the graph filename BARGRAPH.
15. Save the worksheet using the filename E16A.
16. Print the graph PIEGRAPH.
17. Print the graph BARGRAPH.

16B In this exercise, you create, save, and print two graphs.

1. Retrieve the E12B file.
2. Specify the type of graph is line.
3. Define the X data range as the Quarter headings in cells C6 through F6.
4. Designate the first data range (A) as the sales values for Washers in cells C7 through F7.
5. Specify the second data range (B) as the sales values for Dryers.
6. Define the third data range (C) as the sales values for Toasters.
7. Designate the fourth data range (D) as the sales values for Stoves.
8. Specify the first title line for the graph as "Able Appliance Company."
9. Define the second title line for the graph as "Forecast."
10. Designate the Y-axis title to be "($000)."
11. Create legend names for each of the data ranges (A through D).
12. View the graph.
13. Name the graph LINEGRP.

14. Save the graph using the graph filename LINEGRP.
15. Change the type of the graph to bar.
16. View the graph.
17. Name the graph BARGRP.
18. Save the graph using the graph filename BARGRP.
19. Save the worksheet using the filename E16B.
20. Print the graph LINEGRP.
21. Print the graph BARGRP.

Using 1-2-3 Add-in Programs

CONCEPTS This topic introduces some of the add-in programs available in 1-2-3. An add-in program provides additional functionality to the 1-2-3 software. Before an add-in program can be used, it must first be attached to 1-2-3 and then invoked.

Three of the add-in programs available are:

1. Auditor — to analyze the contents of cells in worksheets.
2. Viewer — to view worksheet files prior to retrieving a specific file.
3. WYSIWYG — to improve the appearance of worksheets and graphs.

Using the Auditor Add-in 188

The 1-2-3 Auditor add-in provides you with assistance in analyzing a worksheet and its contents. This add-in can be particularly helpful when you are trying to understand the formulas used in a worksheet completed by another individual. The Auditor add-in can also be helpful when you are trying to find computational errors in a worksheet.

Using the Viewer Add-in 189

In some situations, you may want to browse through your worksheet files before you retrieve a particular worksheet. The Viewer add-in allows you to retrieve, link, or browse through your worksheet files. When you do not remember the name of the file that contains a worksheet that you wish to retrieve, the Viewer add-in can be particularly useful.

Using the WYSIWYG Add-in 189

The WYSIWYG add-in allows you to improve the appearance of your worksheets and graphs. Some of its capabilities are:

1. To include a maximum of eight fonts on any printed document.
2. To bold the contents of cells.
3. To place double underlines on a worksheet.
4. To include various degrees of shading to areas on a worksheet.
5. To draw horizontal and vertical lines.
6. To modify row height and column width.
7. To place a box around one cell or outline a range of cells.

TUTORIAL

In this tutorial, you attach the Auditor, Viewer, and WYSIWYG add-in programs. You then invoke each of the add-in programs and use them.

1 Attach an add-in program. You start by attaching each of the add-in programs. If you do not want to use one of the add-in programs, you do not need to attach the add-in.

Press	/	Activates Main menu.
Press	A	Selects Add-in.
Press	A	Selects Attach.
Type or highlight	AUDITOR.ADN	Specifies Auditor as add-in to attach.
Press	↵ ENTER	Selects Auditor to attach.
Press	↵ ENTER	Specifies "no-key" is used to invoke add-in.
Press	Q	Selects Quit.

TIP After you attach the WYSIWYG add-in, the mouse pointer appears as an arrow rather than as a reverse video box.

The Viewer and WYSIWYG add-in programs are attached in the same manner, except that Viewer and WYSIWYG are selected instead of Auditor. ◀

2 Invoke an add-in. Once an add-in program has been attached, it can be invoked and used.

Press	/	Activates Main menu.
Press	A	Selects Add-in.
Press	I	Selects Invoke.
Type or highlight	AUDITOR	Specifies Auditor as add-in to invoke.
Press	↵ ENTER	Selects Auditor.

The Viewer and WYSIWYG add-in programs are invoked in a similar manner, except that Viewer and WYSIWYG are selected instead of Auditor.

3 Use the Auditor add-in. Before starting this exercise, retrieve the worksheet file REV12. Suppose you would like to know what cells are used to compute the sum for Gross in the Plan Revenue column.

Press	/, A, I	Selects Add-in, Invoke.
Type or highlight	AUDITOR	Specifies Auditor as add-in to invoke.
Press	↵ ENTER	Selects Auditor.

Press	(P)	Selects Precedents.
Type or highlight	cell C16	Specifies C16 as precedent source cell.
Press	(↵ ENTER)	Selects C16 as precedent source cell.
Press	(Q)	Quits Auditor add-in.

Note that the cells C7 through C14 are a different color or appear to be more intense. These cells are used in the computation of cell C16.

4 **Use the Viewer add-in.** Suppose you want to browse through the worksheet files in your current directory and then retrieve a particular file.

Invoke	VIEWER add-in	
Press	(B)	Selects Browse.
Press	(→)	Selects drive A as current directory.
Move	pointer to particular filename	Specifies file to view.
Press	(ESC)	
Press	(R)	Selects Retrieve.
Press	(→)	Selects drive A as current directory. Returns to menu.
Move	pointer to particular filename	Specifies file to view.
Press	(↵ ENTER)	Retrieves file.

Note that the file you selected now appears on your screen.

TIP An alternative method for invoking the WYSIWYG add-in is to type a colon by holding down a Shift key and pressing the : key.

5 **Use the WYSIWYG add-in.** Before starting this exercise, make sure you have retrieved worksheet file REV12. Suppose you want to bold the worksheet title and column headings on the worksheet.

Invoke	WYSIWYG add-in ◄	
Press	(F)	Selects Format.
Press	(B)	Selects Bold.
Press	(S)	Selects Set.
Type or highlight	cells A1 through F5	Specifies range of cells to boldface.
Press	(↵ ENTER)	Bolds contents of selected range of cells.

Note that the worksheet title and column headings appear as bold characters. Do not save and replace the worksheet file REV12. Now you remove the add-ins from your computer's memory.

Press	ALT-F10	Activates the Add-in menu.
Press	C	Selects Clear.
Press	Q	Selects Quit.

PROCEDURE SUMMARY

ATTACHING AN ADD-IN

Activate the Main menu.	/
Select Add-in.	A
Select Attach.	A
Type or highlight the desired add-in name.	(your input)
Select desired add-in.	↵ ENTER
Specify "no-key."	↵ ENTER
Select Quit.	Q

INVOKING AN ADD-IN

Activate the Main menu.	/
Select Add-in.	A
Select Invoke.	I
Type or Highlight the desired add-in name.	(your input)
Select the desired add-in.	↵ ENTER

USING THE AUDITOR ADD-IN

Invoke the Auditor add-in.	/, A, I, AUDITOR, ↵ ENTER
Select menu option desired.	(your input)
Complete the menu sequence.	(your input)

USING THE VIEWER ADD-IN

Invoke the Viewer add-in.	/, A, I, VIEWER, ↵ENTER
Select the menu option desired.	(your input)
Complete the menu sequence.	(your input)

USING THE WYSIWYG ADD-IN

Invoke the WYSIWYG add-in.	/, A, I, WYSIWYG, ↵ENTER
Select the menu option desired.	(your input)
Complete the menu sequence.	(your input)

REMOVING ADD-INS FROM MEMORY

Activate the Add-in menu.	ALT-F10
Select Clear.	C
Select Quit.	Q

EXERCISES

17A Attach the Auditor, Viewer, and WYSIWYG add-in programs.

1. Attach the Auditor add-in program.
2. Attach the Viewer add-in program.
3. Attach the WYSIWYG add-in program.

17B Use the Auditor, Viewer, and WYSIWYG add-in programs.

1. Retrieve the E10B1 file using the Viewer add-in program.
2. Use the WYSIWYG add-in program to bold the worksheet title, column headings, and row labels.
3. Print the worksheet.
4. Use the Auditor add-in program to determine the cells used to compute the total value for sales in the fourth quarter.
5. Use the Viewer add-in program to browse through the worksheet files you have created.
6. Use the Viewer add-in program to retrieve a worksheet file of your choice.

Checkpoint 3

What You Should Know

- ✔ The Worksheet Titles and Worksheet Windows commands make it easier to work with large worksheets.
- ✔ Headers, footers, and borders can be printed for worksheets.
- ✔ Data within a worksheet can be sorted and extracted.
- ✔ A variety of types of graphs can be created and printed.
- ✔ Several add-in programs can be used with 1-2-3 to increase its functionality.

Review Questions

1. What are some of the uses of the Worksheet Titles and Worksheet Windows commands?
2. What is the difference between a header and a footer?
3. How can you print the same row and column text descriptions on each printed page of a large worksheet?
4. For printing purposes, how do you place a page break in a worksheet?
5. What steps are required to sort data in a worksheet?
6. What steps are necessary to extract data from a worksheet?
7. How do you create a graph in 1-2-3?
8. What steps are used to print a graph?
9. What are the basic capabilities of the Auditor, Viewer, and WYSIWYG add-in programs?

CHECKPOINT PROBLEM A

In this problem, you work with an existing worksheet.

1. Retrieve the CP2PA file using the Viewer add-in program.
2. Create a header that places the date at the left side of the header line.
3. Create a footer that centers "Daily Sales" in the footer line.
4. Print the worksheet.
5. Sort the daily sales data so that total sales per day are in descending order.
6. Print the worksheet.
7. Extract the Day and the Sales for each product for the days in which total sales quantities are greater than 315. Place the information on a separate page.
8. Boldface the worksheet title and column headings.
9. Save the worksheet using the filename CP3PA.
10. Print the worksheet.

CHECKPOINT PROBLEM B

In this problem, you work with an existing worksheet.

1. Retrieve the CP2PB file.
2. Create a bar graph for the monthly Sales, Gross Profit, and Net Income data. Include appropriate titles and legend information.
3. Name the graph ABCBAR and save the graph under ABCBAR.
4. Print the ABCBAR graph.
5. Create a line graph for the monthly Sales, Gross Profit, and Net Income data. Include appropriate titles, legend information, and a horizontal grid pattern.
6. Name the graph ABCLINE and save it under ABCLINE.
7. Save the worksheet using the filename CP3PB.
8. Print the ABCLINE graph.

COMPREHENSIVE PROBLEMS

Problem A

In this exercise you create a spreadsheet detailing the projected profits for the XYZ Company over a ten-year period; print the worksheet using a header, borders, and page breaks; then create and print a bar graph.

1. Enter "   XYZ COMPANY" in cell F1.
2. Enter "PROJECTED PROFITS" in cell F2.
3. Enter the column titles (centered) as "YEAR 1" through "YEAR 10" in cells B4 through K4. Follow the YEAR 10 title with "TOTAL" column.
4. Enter the row title "SALES" in cell A6, "TOTAL EXPENSES" in cell A7, "PROFIT BEFORE TAX" in cell A9, "TAXES" in cell A10, and "PROFIT AFTER TAX" in cell A12.
5. Enter the titles "ASSUMPTIONS", "SALES GROWTH RATE", "EXPENSE RATE", and "TAX RATE" in cells A14 through A17.
6. Widen column A to accommodate the longest label.
7. Enter the value ".05" in cell C15 as the SALES GROWTH RATE. Copy the value to cells D15 through K15.
8. Enter the value ".60" in cell B16 as the EXPENSE RATE. Copy the value to cells C16 through K16.
9. Enter the value ".40" in cell B17 as the TAX RATE. Copy the value to cells C17 through K17.
10. SALES are 30,000 in YEAR 1 and are projected to increase by five percent per year for YEAR 2 through YEAR 10. Enter the value "30000" in cell B6 and enter the proper formula in cell C6 for sales in YEAR2.
11. TOTAL EXPENSES are projected to be 60 percent of sales. Enter the proper formula for TOTAL EXPENSES for YEAR 1 in cell B7.
12. PROFIT BEFORE TAX is equal to SALES minus TOTAL EXPENSES. Enter the proper formula in cell B9.
13. TAXES are equal to 40% of PROFIT BEFORE TAX. Enter the proper formula in cell B10.
14. PROFIT AFTER TAX is equal to PROFIT BEFORE TAX minus TAXES. Enter the proper formula in cell B12.
15. Copy the SALES formula for YEAR 2 to YEAR 3 through YEAR 10.
16. Copy the TOTAL EXPENSES, PROFIT BEFORE TAXES, TAXES, and PROFIT AFTER TAX formulas for YEAR 1 to YEAR 2 through YEAR 10.
17. Each entry in the TOTAL column is the sum of YEAR 1 through YEAR 10 for the respective variable. Enter the proper formula for TOTAL SALES in cell L6.
18. Copy the TOTAL formula to the other cells in the TOTAL column.
19. Create a Global Format of comma with zero decimal places.
20. Format the ASSUMPTIONS range of cells for a percent format with zero decimal places.

21. Place single underlines in cells B8 through L8 and cells B11 through L11.
22. Place a double underline in cells B13 through L13.
23. Specify column A as a border to be printed on each page.
24. Create a header with "XYZ COMPANY" left aligned and the page number right aligned.
25. Print the ASSUMPTIONS on a separate page, but do not place the page break in column A.
26. Print the worksheet.
27. Save the worksheet using the filename PROFITS.
28. Retrieve the file PROFITS.
29. Create a bar graph that includes SALES, PROFIT BEFORE TAX, and PROFIT AFTER TAX for YEAR 1 through YEAR 10.
30. Enter XYZ COMPANY as the first title line and PROJECTED PROFITS as the second title line.
31. Enter DOLLARS as the y-axis title.
32. Create a legend for the graph.
33. View the graph.
34. Name the graph PROFBAR and save it using the graph filename PROFBAR.
35. Save the worksheet using the filename PROFITS.
36. Print the PROFBAR graph.

Problem B

In this exercise you print a worksheet using a header, borders, and page break.

1. Retrieve the PROFITS file.
2. Specify column A as a border to be printed on each page.
3. Create a header with "XYZ COMPANY" left aligned and the page number right aligned.
4. Print the ASSUMPTIONS on a separate page (do not place the page break in column A).
5. Boldface the worksheet titles, column titles, and row labels.
6. Print the worksheet.
7. Save the worksheet using the filename PROFITS.

Problem C

In this exercise, you create and print a bar graph.

1. Retrieve the PROFITS file.
2. Create a bar graph that includes SALES, PROFIT BEFORE TAX and PROFIT AFTER TAX for YEAR 1 through YEAR 10.
3. Enter XYZ COMPANY as the first title line.

4. Enter PROJECTED PROFITS as the second title line.
5. Enter DOLLARS as the y-axis title.
6. Create a legend for the graph.
7. Name the graph PROFBAR.
8. Save the graph as PROFBAR.
9. Save the worksheet using the filename PROFITS.
10. Print the PROFBAR graph.

Problem D

In this exercise, you create a worksheet that includes address information for several people and sort the data on the individuals by city and last name.

1. Enter "XYZ COMPANY" in cell B1.
2. Enter "LAST NAME" in cell A5.
3. Enter "FIRST NAME" in cell B5.
4. Enter "CITY" in cell C5.
5. Enter "STATE" in cell D5.
6. Change the column width of column A to 11 characters.
7. Change the column width of column B to 11 characters.
8. Change the column width of column C to 14 characters.
9. Change the column width of column D to 5 characters.
10. Enter the last names "Smith," "Jones," "Adams," "Gomez," "Jones," and "Brown" in cells A6 through A11.
11. Enter the first names "Helen," "Eric," "Mark," "Linda," "Elizabeth," and "Joseph" in cells B6 through B11.
12. Enter the cities "St. Louis," "Chicago," "San Francisco," "Chicago," "San Francisco," and "St. Louis," in cells C6 through C11.
13. Enter the state abbreviations "MO," "IL," "CA," "IL," "CA," and "MO" in cells D6 through D11.
14. Save the worksheet file using the name PEOPLE.
15. Print the worksheet.
16. Sort the PEOPLE file by city and then last name in alphabetical order.
17. Save the worksheet using the filename PEOPLE1.
18. Print the worksheet.

Problem E

In this exercise you find and copy data that satisfy a specific criteria.

1. Retrieve the PEOPLE file.
2. For each individual living in St Louis, extract the LAST NAME and FIRST NAME. Place this information below the worksheet.
3. Save the worksheet using the filename PEOPLE2.
4. Print the worksheet.

Index